Kwame Nkrumah's Political Kingdom and Pan-Africanism Reinterpreted, 1909–1972

African Governance, Development, and Leadership

Series Editor: Sabella O. Abidde, Alabama State University

Advisory Board: Getachew Metaferia, Georges Nzongola-Ntalaja, Adebayo Oyebade, Gloria Chuku, Gorden Moyo, and Olubukola Stella Adesina

The African Governance, Development, and Leadership series identifies and elaborates on the strategic place of governance, development, and leadership within African studies. Reflecting the fact that life in Africa continues to change; particularly in political, development, and socio-economic arenas; this series explores issues focusing on the ongoing mobilization for good governance, viable and impartial institutions, and the search for sustainable and economic development. Addressing gaps and larger needs in the developing scholarship on Africa and the African diaspora, this series publishes scholarly monographs and edited collections in the humanities, social science, and social scientific traditions.

Recent Titles

Kwame Nkrumah's Political Kingdom and Pan-Africanism Reinterpreted, 1909–1972 by A.B. Assensoh and Yvette M. Alex-Assensoh

Africa in the Twenty-First Century: The Promise of Development and Democratization edited by Gashawbeza Bekele and Adebayo Oyebade

Nigeria-United States Relations 1960–2016 by Olayiwola Abegunrin

The Illusion of the Post-Colonial State: Governance and Security Challenges in Africa by W. Alade Fawole

Africans and the Exiled Life: Migration, Culture, and Globalization edited by Sabella Ogbobode Abidde and Brenda I. Gill

Kwame Nkrumah's Political Kingdom and Pan-Africanism Reinterpreted, 1909–1972

A.B. Assensoh and
Yvette M. Alex-Assensoh

LEXINGTON BOOKS
Lanham • Boulder • New York • London

Published by Lexington Books
An imprint of The Rowman & Littlefield Publishing Group, Inc.
4501 Forbes Boulevard, Suite 200, Lanham, Maryland 20706
www.rowman.com

86-90 Paul Street, London EC2A 4NE, United Kingdom

Copyright © 2022 by The Rowman & Littlefield Publishing Group, Inc.

All rights reserved. No part of this book may be reproduced in any form or by any electronic or mechanical means, including information storage and retrieval systems, without written permission from the publisher, except by a reviewer who may quote passages in a review.

British Library Cataloguing in Publication Information Available

Library of Congress Cataloging-in-Publication Data

Names: Assensoh, A. B., author. | Alex-Assensoh, Yvette M., author.
Title: Kwame Nkrumah's political kingdom and pan-Africanism reinterpreted, 1909–1972 / A.B. Assensoh, Yvette M. Alex-Assensoh.
Other titles: African governance, development, and leadership.
Description: Lanham : Lexington Books, 2022. | Series: African governance, development, and leadership | Includes bibliographical references and index. | Summary: "This book provides an in-depth study of the life of the late Pan-African leader Kwame Nkrumah. The authors present a twenty-first-century reinterpretation of Nkrumah's Pan-Africanist views in the context of Black unity as well as Black liberation within the African continent and the United States and Caribbean diaspora"—Provided by publisher.
Identifiers: LCCN 2021053833 (print) | LCCN 2021053834 (ebook) | ISBN 9781666906745 (cloth) | ISBN 9781666906769 (paperback) | ISBN 9781666906752 (epub)
Subjects: LCSH: Nkrumah, Kwame, 1909–1972. | Pan-Africanism. | Presidents—Ghana—Biography. | Ghana—Politics and Government—1957–1979.
Classification: LCC DT512.3.N57 A785 2022 (print) | LCC DT512.3.N57 (ebook) | DDC 966.705092 [B]—dc23/eng/20211209
LC record available at https://lccn.loc.gov/2021053833
LC ebook record available at https://lccn.loc.gov/2021053834

In his lifetime, Ghana's late president Osagyefo *Dr. Kwame Nkrumah (1909–1972) styled his ideas and principles as* Nkrumaism. *He, in fact, established the erstwhile Kwame Nkrumah Ideological Institute at Winneba, Central Region of Ghana—headed as director at the time by Mr. Kodwo Addison (1927–1985)—to promote Nkrumaism. This book is dedicated partly to the adherents as well as to the admirers of the Ghanaian political leader in Africa and in the worldwide Black Diaspora, including those with whom we met and broke bread in Europe, North America, the Caribbean, and Southeast Asia.*

And

Also, to the Assensoh (or Assenso) and Alex Families of Ghana and USA.

Contents

Foreword		ix
Preface		xxi
Acknowledgments		xxix
Chronology of Kwame Nkrumah		xxxv
1	Birth, Early Education, and Employment	1
2	Overseas Student Years: Nkrumah's American and UK Sojourns, 1935–1947	5
3	Kwame Nkrumah and Pan-Africanism: A New Interpretation	21
4	Years of Activism and Postcolonial Gold Coast, 1947–1960	59
5	Ghana: Kwame Nkrumah's Political Kingdom, 1960–1966	75
Epilogue: The 1966 Coup, Exile, Death, and Cultural Legacy of Kwame Nkrumah		83
Appendix: The OAU Charter		107
Bibliography		109
Index		113
About the Authors		121

Foreword

Ghana's Kwame Nkrumah: A Man of Faith and Politics

Damien Ejigiri

Dean, The Nelson Mandela College of Government and Social Science, Southern University, and A&M College

> Azikiwe utilized religious colleges for his learning, studying theology and at times preached in some African American Churches. Nkrumah did the same. Nnamdi Azikiwe and Kwame Nkrumah utilized religion in various ways toward enhancing [of] their ability to cope and adapt in America.[1]
>
> —Toyin Falola and Niyi Afolabi,
> *African Minorities in the New World*

In a large measure, this publication provides a 21st-century re-interpretation of Ghana's late president Kwame Nkrumah's life, times, and his notion of Pan-Africanism. Also, it is well established by Professors A.B. Assensoh and Yvette M. Alex-Assensoh, as co-authors—with a lot of historicity, Afrocentric and political insights—that there is a lot to learn anew about Ghana's first elected indigenous citizen as prime minister in 1957 and, three years later (on July 1, 1960), as postcolonial Ghana's first republican president Kwame Nkrumah, a foremost Pan-Africanist.

Most certainly, as an African scholar myself, this indeed is a topic, with which I am very familiar and, as a result, I feel deeply honored that the co-authors have once again invited me to provide this foreword. As I still recall vividly and with a lot of pleasure, I provided a similar foreword to their co-authored book *Malcolm X And Africa*, published in 2016 by Cambria Press of Amherst, New York.

As well captured in this publication in various segments, it is very fascinating that the two future West African political leaders—my fellow Igbo compatriot, the late Dr. Nnamdi Azikiwe of Nigeria and the late president Kwame Nkrumah of Ghana—would play major nationalist roles in the former Gold Coast (now Ghana) and Nigeria, respectively. Their paths first crossed in the former Gold Coast in the 1920s, when Dr. Azikiwe, a Nigerian citizen and future anti-colonialist nationalist leader, was a newspaper publisher and editor. What is equally fascinating, as quoted above, was the fact that both Azikiwe and Nkrumah, as students in the United States, in strikingly very different periods, were staunch Christians. Specifically, as also confirmed in the available records, the two West Africans—who were at the time in search of the proverbial golden fleece, or higher education—were very disciplined church-going Christians in those earlier years, as students at Lincoln University, a Historically Black College and University (HBCU) in Pennsylvania, "founded in 1854, [and] was the first institution [of higher learning] in the United States to give higher education to Negroes [African-Americans] and to train these students for service and leadership within the Negro population of the States."[2]

Very uniquely, both future African leaders—Ghana's late president Nkrumah (1909–1972), and Nigerian president Azikiwe (1904–1996)—were given Christian names at birth, which they would later, in their lives as foreign students, change in order to adopt their indigenous African first names. For example, Ghana-born Nkrumah was named Francis when baptized as a Roman Catholic but as Ghana's first elected indigenous president, he was known as Kwame Nkrumah; however, he was famously referred to by his supporters as the Osagyefo, which meant a warrior, who fought and won over British colonial rule. Then, the late president Nnamdi Azikiwe of Nigeria (1904–1996) was also named Benjamin at birth in his native Eastern Nigeria in colonial Nigeria, my own Igbo region of Nigeria. Also, Dr. Azikiwe was only five years older than Ghana's Dr. Nkrumah, but their biographical trajectory is fascinatingly similar. Azikiwe, who changed his first name to Nnamdi by choice, for example, was Nigeria's first indigenous governor-general and, later ceremonial president. Both men, who were America-educated, later led their respective nations as their first presidents.

Being older, Nnamdi Azikiwe was the first to attend Pennsylvania-based Lincoln University and University of Pennsylvania, respectively, indeed much earlier than Nkrumah did. As their fate and fortunes would have it, the facts are that it was after returning from America as a practicing journalist to the then Gold Coast (renamed Ghana at independence in 1957) and, indeed, also as a publisher that Nigeria-born Azikiwe influenced Nkrumah, invariably for the latter—as a trained indigenous school teacher in the Gold Coast—to start thinking about going to America to follow the intellectual footsteps of Azikiwe in search of higher education. Nkrumah confirmed that he decided to follow the academic example of the Nigerian nationalist-*cum*-politician, who impressed him in two significant ways: through his published articles and also when he addressed their then Gold Coast Teachers' Association.[3]

In his own words, Nkrumah, the future Ghanaian president, *inter alia*, wrote in 1957:

> My nationalism was also revived at about that time through articles written in *The African Morning Post* by Nnamdi Azikiwe, a Nigerian from Onitsha Azikiwe was himself a graduate of an American University and, when I had first met him he told me, thus after he had addressed a meeting of the Gold Coast Teachers' Association. Some years earlier in Accra, I had been greatly impressed by him and had been more determined than ever to go to America [to study].[4]

Furthermore, the same Azikiwe had given Nkrumah either the encouragement or impetus to travel to America, especially as he scribbled in a note he had left for Nkrumah in the cabin of his sailing boat, a UK-bound ship in 1935. At Lincoln University, Nkrumah would stay for two academic degrees, while pursuing three others—including an unfinished doctoral degree in Philosophy, whereby he had only a dissertation to complete and earn it—at University of Pennsylvania. Instead, as he wrote at the time, after falling very ill from the bitter cold, he did realize how very close he had been to dying that day. Therefore, his resolve, after waking up from bed, was that he "had made up my mind that I would leave America and return home so soon as ever this could be arranged [to return to the Gold Coast]."[5]

THE EARLIER ROLE OF RELIGION IN NKRUMAH'S LIFE

It is, indeed, very traditional that when young, several of us, as Africans, were taken to church and, later to Christian schools. That is why it is not strange that, in his earlier years back in the Gold Coast, where he interacted often with Christian missionaries, Nkrumah was fixated on the Roman Catholic religion, as he attended its elementary schools back in his birthplace in colonial Gold Coast. In fact, there were rumors that Nkrumah once entertained the idea of becoming a Catholic priest; whether that was on his mind or not, what seemed to have saved him from that thought was his earlier thoughts in life about religion, money, and also women in general. He confessed in his published autobiography:

> And I have the same feelings about money and organized and obligatory religion. All three of them represent, to my mind, something that should play a very minor part in a man's life, for once one of them gets the upper hand, man becomes a slave and his personality is crushed.[6]

In spite of Nkrumah's, sometimes, ambivalence toward the Christian religion, he still confessed that he almost embraced Catholicism's Jesuit Order, especially after he accepted to become a lay teacher (or tutor) in the first Roman Catholic Seminary established to produce indigenous priests to serve Catholic churches and educational institutions throughout the former Gold Coast, which was at the time under British colonial rule and, as a result, had several Irish and other foreign priests to serve their church. The future Ghanaian leader's further confirmation of his obvious interest in the Jesuit Order was couched in the following words:

> I regained my religious fervor to such an extent that I seriously formed the idea of taking the vocation of priesthood myself. I wanted to be a member of the Jesuit Order, and the idea lingered with me for a whole year. Eventually, however, the old desire to be up and doing, to further my education and to proceed to America in order to do this, but the better of me and I felt the walls of the seminary would enclose me for life if I didn't soon take action.[7]

Apart from Nkrumah temporarily minimizing his fascination with religion earlier in his life to concentrate in his teacher training education at Achimota College and also to succeed later as a trained teacher, Professors Toyin Falola and Niyi Afolabi, in the opening quote from *African Minorities in the New World* (2008) have confirmed that both Nkrumah and his Nigerian mentor Dr. Nnamdi Azikiwe, as students in America, did not shy away from openly patronizing the Christian protestant churches in Pennsylvania in a variety of ways, mainly to raise the much-needed funds to help them cope financially and otherwise.[8] Nkrumah, for example, was forced by immigration rules to be in school at all times after earning his first degree, the Bachelor of Arts in Economics and Sociology in 1939 from Lincoln University. Therefore, for immigration reasons, in the same year (1939), he enrolled in the Lincoln Theological Seminary, while also continuing his graduate studies in Philosophy and Education at the University of Pennsylvania. Nkrumah in his published memoir confirmed, below, that he revisited his interest in Christian preaching when he was in the Seminary as, among other details, he wrote:

> While I was studying theology at Lincoln Seminary, I spent much of my free time preaching in Negro churches. Almost every Sunday, I was booked to preach at some church or other and I really enjoyed doing it. I had made many friends, for the Negro churches play the part of community centers more than most places of worship. It was after I had been preaching in a Baptist Church in Philadelphia that I was introduced to Portia and her sister Romana. They invited me back to their house for dinner, and from that time on a strong friendship existed among the three of us.[9]

Foreword

NKRUMAH'S IDEOLOGICAL INTERESTS AND INFLUENCES AS A STUDENT IN AMERICA

It is very significant for me to note that several scholars of Africa have taken the time to capture the essence of Nkrumah's Pan-Africanist interests, as well as promotion of the concept that was initially introduced by Caribbean-born George Padmore, who was a very good friend of Nkrumah when he moved to the colonial capital of London from the United States of America. Most certainly, co-authors Assensoh and Alex-Assensoh have taken the time to provide their readers with a very detailed analysis of Pan-Africanism in chapter 3 of this book. However, sometimes, what has not been shown adequately by others is also the fact that as Nkrumah confirmed in his memoir in 1957 (republished in 1972) he underwent a lot of influences as a student in America. For example, from the perspective of the sociology that he studied as part of his undergraduate degree's double major (together with economics), his main pre-occupation ideologically, during his student years, centered on two sociological schools of thought; indeed, he named them in his own words:

> One [of the schools of thought] represented by the Howard [University] Sociologists, led by Professor [E. Franklin] Fraser, and the other led by Dr. M.J. Herzkovits, professor of Anthropology at Northwestern University. The Howard School of Thought maintained that the Negro in America had completely lost his [or her] cultural contact with Africa, and the other school [of thought], led by Herzkovits, maintained that there were still African survivals in the United States, and that the Negro of America had in no way lost his cultural contact with the African continent. I supported, and still support the latter view and I went on one occasion to Howard University to defend it.[10]

Furthermore, Nkrumah confirmed in his own words how he tried his best to get acquainted with many political organizations while still in America, including the Democrats, Republicans, the Communists, and the Trotskyites. According to him, "It was in connection with the last movement that I met one of its leading members, Mr. C.L.R. James, and through him, I learned how an underground movement worked."[11] While the future Ghanaian leader acquired diverse knowledge from all sources, he explained that he "concentrated on finding a formula by which the whole colonial question and the problem of imperialism could be solved."[12]

While all of the foregoing factors show readers several aspects of the concrete measures Nkrumah, as a college student in America, adopted to enrich his mind, other analyses by the authors provide much valuable information about Nkrumah in this new study of his life and times. Very significantly, the ardent Pan-Africanist (Nkrumah) returned to the former Gold Coast (whose name he would help to change to Ghana) to participate actively in the decolonization struggle that had been started by leaders of the foremost nationalist organization known as the UGCC. Interestingly, just like our own Nigeria, the colonial administrators did not permit the use of the words political parties at the time. What is interesting is the fact that, in the end, Nkrumah broke away from the UGCC, formed his own organization that he cleverly called the Convention People's Party (CPP), thereby unilaterally creating a political party as such. His trick worked because, through the CPP, he won subsequent national elections and, in the end, he led Ghana as Leader of Government Business, a *de facto* prime minister title (pre-independence); as well as being named the substantive prime minister (1957–1960); and finally, as Ghana's president, under the country's first republican constitution through which Nkrumah, as the elected president, ruled Ghana from July 1, 1960 to February 24, 1966, when his government was overthrown in a *coup d'etat*.[13]

Indeed, I always remember that Nkrumah's overthrow in the 1966 coup took place barely a month after Nigeria's own successful *coup d'etat* of January 15, 1966, two events that took the citizens of both countries by surprise. That was especially so, since no such event ever took place in which politicians as well as military men and women were killed. Nkrumah was out of Ghana and, as a result, was not harmed personally; Nigerian prime minister Alhaji Tafawa Balewa as well as his 1960–1966 Finance Minister Festus Okotie-Eboh, Western regional governor Samuel Akintola, and few other military leaders were killed for the coup to succeed.

Indeed, those who knew Nkrumah well did agree that, from the year of his birth (1909) in the small town of Nkroful in the Western Region of the Gold Coast (Ghana) to the year of his death (1972) in Bucharest, Romania, his life had been full of very interesting scenarios, as this book has cataloged in a very fascinating way. For example, he seemed to have lived according to his dictate that money should not play a big part in his affairs as a human being. Otherwise, as discussed in this book, one would wonder how he had to rely on an UGCC leader (Dr. Danquah) to get money to pay for his shipping fare from Liverpool, UK to the then Gold Coast to serve as the general secretary of the movement? Furthermore, when he was offered the UGCC position, which would give him a salary and a car to use for his work, the future president of Ghana did not display any excitement as expected. Instead, he, among other details, wrote:

> He [Ako Adjei] had recommended to the Executive Committee [of the U.G.C.C.] that I should be invited to become general secretary. He added that the executive Committee had offered to pay me one hundred pounds a month and to provide me with a car. The money and the car didn't interest me so much. The job of general secretary, however, most certainly did.[14]

Foreword

THE SURPRISE AT NKRUMAH'S OVERTHROW

Looking at statements like the one quoted above, from his published 1957 memoirs, which was re-issued in 1972, it did not sit well with several very young Africans, like myself, who heard a lot about Nkrumah's Ghana, with its free education in elementary and secondary schools. It was hard for us, in Nigeria, to hear that Nkrumah and his cabinet members as well as the ruling CPP's top leadership were all corrupt, hence the coup took place in 1966. My father, back in Igboland in the then Eastern Nigeria and some of our elders were disturbed that, in Nkrumah's case, an Apaloo Assets Commission was set up to probe his assets, in fact starting with examining the contents of the deposed leader's three last testaments (or wills) and final codicils, which we read that he did make changes in the wills.

As the co-authors of this book have pointed out elsewhere in this text, the same Nkrumah, barely a year or two after he won national elections to become the first elected president of Ghana, made his famous early morning broadcast—known as the "Dawn Broadcast"—to decry rampant greed and corruption among top political party members and some governmental officials. If so, just four years later in February 1966, some of us in Nigeria wondered: How did the sanctimonious-sounding President Nkrumah suddenly become so corrupt? Some of us, as young Africans, impressed with his ideas, pondered deeply, but we were too young to do anything. However, the Nigerian and Ghanaian coups prompted several of us to start following African politics to know more.

Also, watching events from our safe havens at home, we could not make either judgments or accusatory statements when it came to Ghanaian issues. After all, it was not only Ghana but also our own Nigeria that had tasted its very first military overthrow. Thankfully, post-Nkrumah Ghana, even under military dictatorship known as the National Liberation Council (NLC), seemed as stable and peaceful as anticipated. For the future, when there was the promise to elect politicians in 1969 to rule Ghana, our prayer was that the country would remain so for the NLC leaders to hand power over peacefully to elected politicians! Nigerians like my young self were fascinated to follow Ghana's politics. Therefore, we were happy to learn that the succeeding civilian regime, which lasted from 1969 to 1972, was headed by a very well-educated scholar, the late prime minister Kofi A. Busia (1913–1978). Dr. Busia, a University of London- and Oxford-educated scholar, and also a professor of sociology, was well known for his fierce opposition to Nkrumah and his government. Heavily courted by a section of the NLC military regime, Dr. Busia formed his Progress Party (PP) to contest the general elections. His own major opponent was Mr. K.A. Gbedemah, who hailed from the ethnic Ewe group of the assassinated coup leader General Kotoka, and a former finance minister of Ghana under the Nkrumah regime, who deserted the Nkrumah regime to live in exile in Europe until the 1966 coup.

Following post-Nkrumah Ghana was very fascinating for me. For example, in the 1969 general elections, Professor Busia—who had become very popular in West Africa—was the head of the victorious political party, and he was slated to become the prime minister with executive powers. The position of president, without executive powers, went to former Chief Justice Edward Akufo-Addo, who had chaired the Constitutional Commission to draft a new constitution for Ghana. Unfortunately, the 1969–1970 Busia-Akufo-Addo regime suffered a January 13, 1972 military overthrow, which was led by the then Colonel Ignatius Kutu Acheampong. At the time, the deposed prime minister Busia, known to be a diabetic, was reported to be in the United Kingdom for medical treatment. Also Ghana's deposed president Nkrumah, now in exile in Sekou Toure's Guinea, and his supporters had the last laugh that while he ruled Ghana under various titles from the mid-1950s to 1966, his arch political opponent (Dr. Busia) ruled Ghana for barely three years (1969–1972). As young admirers of Nkrumah, some of us, along with some political observers, wondered if the deposed president Nkrumah would be invited back home by Colonel Acheampong and his National Redemption Council (NRC). As it is common knowledge, that did not happen; instead, a few weeks later (on April 27, 1972), Nkrumah died of cancer at a Bucharest medical clinic in Romania.

Personally, I still have an admiration for Ghana as the first British colony in Africa to attain national independence because of the very hard nationalist battle waged by Nkrumah and his political allies. It is interesting to note that the son of the late president Akufo-Addo—Nana Dankwa Akufo-Addo, a trained Lawyer—is now the president of Ghana. He and his New Patriotic Party (NPP) regime were up for re-election in the Fall of 2020, and they won. It had been reported in the international press that he handled the coronavirus pandemic in such admirable manner that many of his Ghanaian compatriots expected him to succeed in being re-elected for his second and last term as president of Ghana.

FRIENDS OF GHANA AND AFRICA

There are many foreign friends of Ghana and Africa, who follow news about the geographic region. Some of them, including myself, subscribe to such Pan-Africanist publications as the New York–based *Africa Watch Magazine,* which was brought to our attention by co-authors Assensoh (A.B.) and Alex-Assensoh (Yvette). From the well-edited publication, those of us living in America are able to follow events in Africa in general, but

Nigeria and Ghana in particular. While wishing both countries well, we particularly prayed that there would be peace during Ghana's Fall 2020 general elections. Following African politics, as keen Pan-African observers, we always wished that the various electoral processes would be as free and fair as in Western elections. In fact, while Nkrumah's popularity, back in the former Gold Coast, propelled him to several electoral victories, just as the co-authors have discussed elsewhere in this book, it is also a fact that several incumbent African leaders tended to perpetuate their rule or leadership through rigged elections. Such unfortunate situations often led to military intervention in the political process. However, in places that electoral processes seemed to be fair, there were other actions on the part of politicians,. which often led to instability and, as a result, also military intervention in the political process. My prayer is that all such coup-inviting situations will end very fast.

In postcolonial Africa, some of us—with Pan-Africanist interests—looked on helplessly when some leaders tried to declare themselves presidents-for-Life. Also, some of them banned political opposition and instituted one-party governance. Ghana, under Nkrumah; Malawi, under Hastings Kamuzu Banda (1898–1997); Zimbabwe under Robert Mugabe (1924–2019) and a few other countries were typical examples.

Very interestingly, a few African countries—in addition to South Africa—have remained unscathed by military intervention in their internal affairs. Among the few such nations are the French-speaking African country of Senegal and also Kenya, Zambia, Tanzania, Mozambique, Namibia, Guinea Bissau, and others. Even, Ethiopia, which prided itself as an Empire, with Emperor Haile Selassie (1892–1975) as its long-term monarchical leader, did not survive the military wave. Also, Liberia, which often saw itself as a prototype of American democratic process, saw its own many years of control by emancipated American slaves, who styled themselves as Americo-Liberians, eroded by its own military intervention in April 1980. That was when the then president William R. Tolbert, Jr. was overthrown in a very brutal *coup d'etat* led by Master-Sergeant Samuel K. Doe, an indigenous Liberian member of the country's Armed Forces.

Sadly, unlike Ghana's Nkrumah, who was overthrown in absentia, Liberian president Tolbert was overthrown at dawn, arrested and assassinated at his Executive Mansion in Monrovia, the capital that was named in honor of America's former president James Monroe, who played roles in the work of expeditionary forces of freed slaves, who visited Liberia in search of a new home away from America, where they had suffered enslavement for not less than a century and racism later. Since their arrival in Liberia, which declared itself free and independent in July 1847, the country had always been ruled by members of the Americo-Liberian-controlled True Whig Party.[15]

Ghanaian president Nkrumah had a special affinity with Liberia; for example, on his way from Liverpool to the Gold Coast to work for the UGCC, Liberia was one of the countries he stopped over to visit, apart from Sierra Leone, a former British colony whose capital (Freetown) was established to receive some of the freed slaves from British colonies in the Caribbean. As Ghana's new prime minister in 1957, among the first nations Nkrumah visited was Liberia, where he was welcomed warmly by the then president William V.S. Tubman, Sr. (1895–1971). When Nkrumah was overthrown in 1966, Tubman was still in power in Liberia, having first been elected in 1944; he ruled until he died in office in 1971 soon after surgery in London, United Kingdom.

Indeed, Ghana's history is intertwined in such a way with the history of several of the countries discussed that it often brings back to memory Kwame Nkrumah's independence eve pronouncement on March 6, 1957: "Ghana's independence is meaningless unless it is linked up with the total liberation of Africa."[16] How true, indeed, as it is not very surprising that after Nkrumah's Ghana attained its independence in 1957, it paved the way for several colonized nations on the continent and, also, in Asia—in the context of Afro-Asian solidarity—to gain their own freedom and self-determination. It was, therefore, not surprising that the British Broadcasting Corporation (BBC) surveyed its listeners in Africa, who voted overwhelmingly that Ghana's late president Kwame Nkrumah was their chosen "Man of the millennium."[17]

NOTES

1. Toyin Falola and Niyi Afolabi. 2008. *African Minorities in the New World.* New York & London: Routledge, pp. 88–89.
2. Kwame Nkrumah. 1972. *Kwame Nkrumah: Autobiography of Kwame Nkrumah.* New York: International Publishers, p. 29.
3. Kwame Nkrumah, 1972. Ibid., p. 22.
4. Ibid., p. 22.
5. Ibid., pp. 33–34.
6. Nkrumah, op. cit., p.12.
7. Ibid., p. 22.
8. Toyin Falola and Niyi Afolabi, op. cit., pp. 88–89.
9. Nkrumah, 1972, p. 41.
10. Ibid., p. 44.
11. Ibid., p. 44.
12. Ibid., p. 45.
13. Assensoh, 1998, op. cit., p. 112.
14. Nkrumah, 1972, op. cit., p. 61.
15. Assensoh & Alex-Assensoh. 2016. *Malcolm X And Africa.* Amherst, NY: Cambria Press, pp. 75–76.

16. The quotation was from Nkrumah's 1957 independence day speech, which can be found in the Ghana National Archives in Accra; it is also found in several publications, including Dr. Ama Biney's book, *The Social and Political Thought of Kwame Nkrumah*. Palgrave-Macmillan Publishers, 2011.

17. The BBC honor for Nkrumah, as "Man of the Millennium" took place in the year 2000.

BIBLIOGRAPHY

Assensoh, A.B. & Yvette M. Alex-Assensoh. 2016. *Malcolm X And Africa*. Amherst, N Y: Cambria Press.

Assensoh, A.B. 1998. *Kwame Nkrumah of Africa: His Formative Years and the Beginning of His Political Career, 1935–1948*. Devon, UK: Arthur H. Stockwell Ltd.

Biney, Ama. 2011. *The Social And Political Thought of Kwame Nkrumah*. New York, NY: Palgrave-Macmillan Publishers.

British Broadcasting Corporation (BBC). 2000. "Kwame Nkrumah: Man of The Millennium Award" Broadcast.

Falola, Toyin & Niyi Afolabi. 2008. *African Minorities In The New World*. New York, NY & London: Routledge.

Nkrumah, Kwame. 1972. *Ghana: Autobiography of Kwame Nkrumah*. New York, NY: International Publishers.

Preface

In 1959, in a major speech commemorating the Tenth Anniversary of the CPP, he (Nkrumah) called for the reorganization of the party. Among the announced important organizational changes implemented included the establishment of a youth wing and other auxiliary bodies. Yet, nothing changed. In his famous "Dawn Broadcast" of 1961, Nkrumah was forced to attack the corruption and selfishness of his (CPP) party officials and he announced his intention to take control over the direction of the (political) party.[1]

By July 1961, Ghana's first elected indigenous president Kwame Nkrumah had barely served one year as the country's elected president. However, he had also previously served his fellow countrymen as prime minister of independent Ghana from March 6, 1957 to June 30, 1960. As quoted above, London-based *Third World Book Review* editor Kofi Buenor Hadjor commented on the 1961 "Dawn Broadcast" by Nkrumah, as Ghana's president, in which he scolded his cabinet members for alleged rampant corruption, greed, and graft. Very interestingly Nkrumah had given a similar speech in 1959 barely two years after Ghana's independence. Using it to mark the tenth anniversary the ruling Convention People's Party, the Ghanaian leader "demanded the reorganization of the party to ensure a continuity with the movement's original principles. Important organizational changes were implemented, including the establishment of a youth wing and other auxiliary bodies. Yet, nothing changed."[2]

Indeed, the 1961 broadcast was a desperate effort of the Ghanaian leader to stop what he saw as "corruption and selfishness of party officials and announced his intention to take control over the direction of the party."[3] However, as editor Buenor further spelled out, Nkrumah realized that merely changing the organizational structure of the party was not enough, and that there was also the need for transformation, as he added: "A party of careerists can be nothing but a party of careerists, no matter how many times it is reorganized."[4]

NKRUMAH, AZIKIWE OF NIGERIA, AND THE GHANA OPPOSITION LEADERS

Nkrumah gratefully acknowledged Nigeria's first indigenous president Nnamdi Azikiwe in a mentorship fashion, indeed as an individual, who spurred him on to study in America, eventually earning degrees from Lincoln University as well as the University of Pennsylvania, both in Pennsylvania. In fact, from the very day he boarded the ship, in 1935, to leave for America, via the United Kingdom, Nkrumah regarded Dr. Azikiwe as a mentor, who meant a lot to him. For, it was the Nigerian journalist and, later, nationalist, who ignited his interest in American education after he had addressed the Gold Coast Teachers Association, of which Nkrumah was a member as a trained teacher. Today, Ghana owes a major part of its history, including the changing of the colonial name of the Gold Coast to Ghana, to Nkrumah and a few other anti-colonial nationalists and non-violent agitators.

Sadly, Nkrumah was confronted with varied teething problems initially, when he assumed the new country's leadership, earlier as Leader of Government Business (1951–1957), later as prime minister (March 6, 1957–June 30, 1960), and then as the elected president of Ghana (July 1, 1960–February 24, 1966). As several commentators have confirmed, a lot was expected of Nkrumah and his various indigenous postcolonial administrations; at the same time, his opponents were anxious either to undermine or wreck his leadership. An example was how his earlier home in Accra was bombed, but Nkrumah escaped unhurt. The National Liberation Movement (NLM), which opposed Nkrumah's attempts to unify the people of the Gold Coast, embarked on a campaign to organize Asante [Ashanti] cocoa farmers to oppose Nkrumah government's attempts to cut down diseased cocoa trees. Since Nkrumah was preaching unitary state, as against federalism, he willy-nilly ran against the wishes of the NLM, which was determined to achieve its secessionist aim.[5]

In the end, Nkrumah overcame the initial internal problems that he faced, most of which emanated from the quarters of his political opponents of the NLM. Yet, he worked very hard to be able to achieve a lot for Ghana in the areas of education and infrastructure, including the construction of the famous Tema Motorway, seen by many observers and by even his political critics as the best road ever constructed in Ghana. As Dr. Dokutsey described, "The excitement, which caught the people of the Gold Coast at the upcoming of independence [and later republican] celebrations was indescribable."[6]

NKRUMAH: FROM LEADERSHIP TO HIS DOWNFALL, 1951–1966

In spite of the then president Nkrumah's efforts to clean house with those two major speeches, including his 1961 famous "Dawn Broadcast" delivered at dawn on that day, his fellow CPP leaders, who were placed in cabinet positions, did not live up to expectation, as several of them amassed wealth in such greedy fashion that, coupled with his own socialist policies, some leaders' country's Armed Forces, made up of the Ghana Army and the Police Service, decided that he must be removed from office and, as was done, to be probed by a commission of enquiry.

As discussed in the epilogue, the then Major Akwasi Amankwaah (A.A.) Afrifa, in *The Ghana Coup* (1966), as far back as in 1962, had plans to storm the Flagstaff House residential home of President Nkrumah with 300 troops under his command from the then Congo to overthrow the government. He wanted to do so, as he felt that it seemed to him that a "military coup was the only course to rescue our people from [Nkrumah's] tyranny and alien ideologies (socialism, etc.)."[7]

When Nkrumah's downfall eventually came on February 24, 1966, it did not surprise many people inside Ghana. The same Afrifa had teamed up with his commanding officer, then Colonel (now General) Emmanuel K. Kotoka, to seize power the way they did. In spite of the dawn broadcasts, in which Nkrumah decried corrupt and greedy practices, it became necessary for investigative assets' commissions to be instituted, to probe Nkrumah's own suspected ill-gotten assets; the Apaloo Assets Commission was set up in June 1966, barely five months after his overthrow. Among what was scrutinized were Nkrumah's wills and last testament, in which he allotted properties to his immediate nuclear family as well as his extended family members, including his mother, who was then very much alive. As confirmed by published findings, there were adverse findings against Nkrumah and his cabinet members as well as party functionaries by the various assets' commissions.[8]

ATTEMPTS TO REINSTATE NKRUMAH, 1967 FAILED COUP

Since Nkrumah's overthrow in February 1966, several unsuccessful attempts were made either by his agents in Ghana or from his exile ranks in Guinea to reinstate him as Ghana's president. The most serious of these attempts has been discussed by Dr. Woeli Dokutsey in the following words:

> There was the constant fear that Kwame Nkrumah might come back one day.
>
> The state of fear grew more, especially when some three army officers of the Recce Regiment, namely Lt. S.B. Arthur, Lt. Moses Yeboah and Second Lt. E. Osei Poku attempted a counter-coup to oust the NLC from power in [April] 1967. The abortive coup resulted in the death of Lt.-General E.K. Kotoka, who was killed at the Accra Airport (which presently bears his name). Two of the three army officers were shot at the Teshie Firing Range while Second-Lieutenant. E. Osei Poku was sentenced to 30 years' imprisonment.[9]

As expected, the 1967 abortive coup did give a lot of hope to Nkrumah that, one day, his admirers and supporters could help his return to power in Ghana from his Guinean exile. From his Villa Sylli residence in the Guinean capital of Conakry, Nkrumah and his accompanying security detail continued the plan to unseat the NLC and return to Ghana "in order to pursue his aborted attempts to achieve the dream of a united Africa."[10] All of Nkrumah's strenuous efforts to return to power in Ghana were thwarted by the ruling NLC and its intelligence services. For example, after the 1967 abortive coup, one of his top security operatives by the name of Boye Moses was sent to the Republic of Benin, the former Dahomey, to plot for another coup with other operatives of the deposed president. This time, the plan could not be hatched because Moses was intercepted by NLC intelligence officers, who promptly sent him to Ghana, where they "caged him like a zoo animal and paraded him in disgrace [in the cage] through the streets of Accra."[11]

Interestingly, it was also a fact that the NLC leadership back in Ghana also conspired, on several occasions with the country's intelligence agencies, to unsuccessfully get rid of the exiled Nkrumah in Guinea, including efforts to try to assassinate him. For example, the NLC leadership ruling Ghana announced a prize for his capture, dead or alive:

The Ghanaian authorities had placed a reward of $10,000 on Nkrumah's head.

> This bait attracted considerable interest among mercenaries. It happened that a boatful of Ghanaian "fishermen" was spotted well within Guinean territorial waters. The suspicious-looking men were arrested. Upon interrogation, it was discovered that they were not really fishermen but actually security agents sent by the new rulers of Ghana. What was amazing was their knowledge of the layout of Villa Sylli, where Nkrumah was staying. Their plan was either to kidnap

or kill Kwame Nkrumah. Then began a battle of wits between the new Ghana regime and Nkrumah as to who would eliminate the other.[12]

In the end, Nkrumah decided to concentrate on writing books, in which he exposed Western capitalist plans, "plans about how best to liberate Africa from colonial domination. This was the time of the 'Cold War' between America and the Soviet Union."[13]

NKRUMAH'S GOVERNMENT, THE UNITED NATIONS, AND AFRICAN WOMEN'S EMANCIPATION

University of Ghana's professor of Linguistics, Dr. Florence Abena Dolphyne, was among the many young female Ghanaians, who benefited tremendously from Kwame Nkrumah's leadership. This was in tandem with his government's interests in making sure that women were given the chance to develop intellectually and otherwise. It was, therefore, not surprising that after earning her doctoral (PhD) degree in 1965 in Linguistics from School of Oriental and African Studies (SOAS) of the University of London, Dr. Dolphyne returned to Ghana to play a transparent public role at the University of Ghana at Legon, near Accra, the capital of the country; eventually, she rose through the ranks to become a full professor and, in the end, Pro-Vice Chancellor of the university. In *The Emancipation of Women: An African Perspective* (1991), she devoted an entire chapter to the progress that African women have made, which was sub-titled "The Way Forward [for women]."[14] According to Professor Dolphyne, at the end of the United Nations' Decade for women, in 1985, many people were disappointed—and justifiably so—"at how little progress had been made in realizing the objectives of the Decade."[15] Dr. Dolphyne pointed out also in her book how some people were worried by the fact that the end of the UN Decade would mean an end to the focus on women's issues and, as a result, basically an end to the commitment on the part of respective African governments and international agencies which were working to bring about the realization of the total emancipation of African women.[16] Dolphyne also discussed the view of the optimists at the same issue involving African women. She explained further:

> The optimists felt differently. They agreed that the achievements of the Decade had, in some areas, fallen far short of the great expectations that the period had help for many. . . . The Decade had succeeded in creating among men and women throughout the world a keen awareness of the plight of women and, what is more important, a willingness to do something about it.[17]

Dolphyne applauded the fact that when the United Nations declared 1975 as International Women's Year, it "also enjoined member-states to set up national machineries, which would, among other things, study the conditions of women, initiate programs to promote the emancipation of women, and monitor progress made in this direction."[18] Also, Dr. Dophyne put it best as she wrote, among other details, in the conclusion of the third chapter of her book:

> It is said that a journey of a thousand miles begins with the first step. For many rural African women, the United Nations' Decade for Women gave them the opportunity to take a first giant step on the long road to emancipation. The Decade succeeded in creating in them a keen awareness of the unfair subordinate position that society has imposed on women, and in motivating them to do something about it.[19]

Among the salient suggestions that Professor Dolphyne made, a part of her conclusion, was this final statement:

> Above all, women, especially the educated, privileged women, must take active part in programs for the less fortunate women in their communities in order to help them [to] increase their pace and catch up with them, for there is urgent need for all of us to ensure that we reach the end of the long journey to emancipation in the not-too-distant future.[20]

Discussing Ghana's late president Kwame Nkrumah, his political party (the CPP), and the plight of women in Ghana, in particular, but African women in general, Editor Hadjor pointed out how new political attitudes should reflect a new approach toward the position of women, adding:

> The party can't simply talk about the question of women; it must show, through its own actions, that it is prepared to take the lead. . . . Party members must set a personal example and backward, anti-women views must be confronted, exposed and isolated. If this battle is consistently waged, then a climate which is hospitable to women will be established.[21]

Hadjor argued that there would not be a justification for excluding a country's women, in Africa, from national leadership. According to him, "women leaders are the clearest guarantee of equal access to power. A party led by women and men can serve to anticipate the society of the future. Africa will be twice the stronger for that!"[22]

With respect to the status of women under Nkrumah's leadership in Ghana, Dolphyne, in her 1997 book, has confirmed the commendable role that Nkrumah played, compared to several other postcolonial African leaders:

> Ghana boasts of women in all the major professions: there are women lawyers, judges, doctors, engineers, pilots, University lecturers and professors, bankers, accountants, administrators and so on. These professional women have made—and are still making—valuable contribution to various aspects of national life.[23]

Professor Dolphyne's testimony is exemplary because she was one of the younger generations of Ghanaian women, who returned from studying abroad to postcolonial Ghana to benefit from the exhausted positions that women occupied during Kwame Nkrumah's rule. Her professorial positions included being a full professor of Linguistics as well as serving as the Head of the Department of Linguistics and Dean of Arts. Eventually, she became Pro-Vice Chancellor of University of Ghana; in the last position, she was the effective deputy head of the university. Nationally, in Ghana, Professor Dolphyne was for many years the chairperson of Ghana National Council on Women and Development, which gave her the opportunity to represent Ghana at the United Nations's Decade for Women, which started in 1975.[24]

NOTES

1. Kofi Buenor Hadjor. 1987. *On Transforming Africa: Discourse with Africa's Leaders*. Trenton, NJ: Africa world Press, p. 24.
2. Ibid., p. 24.
3. Ibid., p. 24.
4. Ibid., p. 24.
5. Ibid., pp. 25–26.
6. Ibid., p. 27.
7. Assensoh, 1978, op. cit., p. 50.
8. Assensoh, 1998, p. 112.
9. Wolei Dekutsey. 2012. *Kwame Nkrumah: The Great African*. Accra, Ghana: Woeli Publishing Services, p. 45.
10. Ibid., p. 45.
11. Ibid., p. 45.
12. Ibid., p. 46.
13. Ibid., p. 46.
14. Florence Abena Dolphyne. 1991. *The Emancipation of Women: An African Perspective*. Accra: Ghana University's Press.
15. Ibid., p. 84.
16. Ibid., p. 84.

17. Ibid., p. 84.
18. Ibid., p. 86.
19. Ibid., p. 101.
20. Ibid., pp. 101–102.
21. Hadjor, 1987, op. cit., pp. 109–110.
22. Ibid., p. 110.
23. Dolphyne, op. cit., pp. 45–46.
24. Ibid., p. 105.

Acknowledgments

Several people and institutions are owed thanks and appreciation for the varied roles they played in the work that now constitutes this publication. Interestingly, the people are so many that we cannot name them all. It is very similar with libraries and other institutions. For example, among libraries we promptly want to thank are University of Oregon Library in Eugene, Oregon, the Eugene Public Library and, indeed, the Schomburg Center for Research in Black Culture, a branch of New York Public Library, in Harlem, the Elmer Bobst Library of New York University and several others.

When it comes to individuals and fellow scholars, we promptly wish to thank effusively, with unlimited gratitude, Dr. Toyin Falola, the Jacob and Frances Sanger Mossiker Chair in the Humanities at the University of Texas at Austin who believed in our intellectual abilities and encouraged us to work on the manuscript after a discussion with him. He thought that it was time for a new biographical publication on Nkrumah, which would also do a re-interpretation of his Pan Africanist beliefs.

Most certainly, for the detailed documented foreword to this book, we are eternally grateful to Professor Damien Ejigiri, Dean of the Nelson Mandela College of Government and Social Sciences of Baton Rouge, Louisiana-based Southern University and A&M College. He generously responded positively when we sought his involvement in the book project from the beginning. At the time, he was on a "Heavenly Cloud," as he and Lady Pat Ejigiri were celebrating the birth of their first grandchild, Baby Obinna (Obi), with their unlimited appreciation to the child's parents (SIR Winston and Ijeoma Ejigiri, MD, PhD). Professor Ejigiri, we thank you very much for finding the time to provide the foreword to our book.

Also, we thank several colleagues and family members who showed moral support as we started work on the publication; they include Dr. Augustine

Adu Frimpong of Southern University and A&M College in Baton Rouge, Louisiana, as well as Noah Kankam Kwarteng of Nyansapo University College, a Cape Coast University-affiliated institution in Ghana; and Papa Kwabena Gyasi of the International Monetary Fund (IMF) in Washington, D.C., all of whom called often to check on the progress of the project. Dr. Adu Frimpong played a special role in assembling and collating the endnotes for the publication. We are also very grateful to Dr. Victor Essien, Rector of Nyansapo University College, who was a Young Pioneer member at Adisadel College, when Nkrumah visited the all-boys institution and, as a result, has had personal knowledge of some of the facts discussed in the book about the youth movement and the late president Nkrumah. Discussions with Dr. Essien and his wife, Mrs. Ophelia Essien, who was also a student at Cape Coast-based Holy Child (Catholic) Secondary School and Sister Vida Kwansa of blessed memory, also a Holy Child alumna, provided useful information about the Nkrumah era, which were both very helpful and timely. We are, indeed, grateful to all of them.

In Oregon, several of our colleagues and friends deserve thanks and appreciation, although we have not singled out any individuals, as we do not want to forget anyone in the process. At University of Oregon, we are grateful to Professors Ibrahim Gassama and Kristie Gibson of the School of Law, former Professors of A.B. and professional colleagues of Yvette, who also provided a lot of support as they inquired on our writing projects and showed a lot of interests. We are also grateful to Cedric Skillon, MD, and family (University of Oregon's former Student Success Vice Provost Doneka Scott and Erin Skillon, formerly of South Eugene High School and now at University of Michigan), who also often inquired about our writing projects; we are grateful to the Men's Group of Eugene, to which A.B. belonged, as several members often wanted to know what both of us were up to in scholarship, especially when coronavirus pandemic kept all of us at home in our efforts to avoid catching the virus. Our joke was that we were under "corona imprisonment," which ended up being helpful for us to concentrate on the book project.

For extra coherence, we are grateful to Dr. Bisi Gwamna and Dr. Bitrus Gwamna, Literary Editors in Iowa,. who took a look at the first draft of the book manuscript and offered very helpful suggestions. We are glad that we have recommended their very useful services to several friends and colleagues. Of course, they bear no blame for any shortcoming of the publication!

We, indeed, cannot end our words of gratitude without mentioning several nuclear and extended family members: Kwadwo Alex Stephen Assensoh, Livingston Alex Kwabena Assensoh; Mary Achiaa of Kuwait ("Lady Canada"), and Mrs. Theresah Adu Frimpong, all of whom provided moral support. Dr. Hassan Wahab of University of Ghana; Dean Abdul Mahdi ("Mannan") as well as Provost Angela Owusu Ansah of Ashesi University in Ghana, all of whom also provided moral support in varied ways. It is a blessing to have such very supportive nuclear and extended family members and fellow scholars.

As it is also the case with popular African political leaders, of which Ghana's late president Kwame Nkrumah was one, several writers have often taken the lead in writing about them. With Nkrumah being, indeed, one of them, we have been very fortunate to encounter several publications about him. Therefore, we cannot end this acknowledgment without expressing our deepest appreciation to several pioneering authors, from whose works we drew quotations, with appropriate citations. They, in fact, include Dr. Woeli Dekutsey of Woeli Publishing Services of Ghana. His very concise biography of Dr. Nkrumah and his fellow nationalist leaders, who are styled as the "Big Six," did provide very useful sources that we either cited or had to research further for elaboration in our own book. His "Great Ghanaians for Young Readers" series has provided a very useful service for youngsters in Africa, particularly Ghana.

We are also very grateful to the former Ghanaian leader, the late president Nkrumah who did not shy away from expressing himself on paper. As Ghana's leader, he wrote several very insightful books, including his autobiography *Ghana: The Autobiography of Kwame Nkrumah*, which was first published by Thomas Nelson and Sons of the United Kingdom to mark Ghana's year of independence (1957) but has, since then, been published by several other publishers, including International Publishers of New York, which issued its own second edition in 1972.

During our research about Nkrumah at Lincoln University's Langston Hughes Memorial Library, we were very impressed by the fact that the university's famous alumnus from Ghana (Nkrumah) had carefully autographed for his *alma mater* copies of his published books, which had been shelved in an enviable "Dr. Kwame Nkrumah Section." There were also other Nkrumah memorabilia, including his university admission documents, which we also tapped to supplement our own research sources, including coauthor Assensoh's earlier writings about the late Ghanaian leader, the earliest of which was the slim but a very tantalizing monograph *Kwame Nkrumah: Six Years in Exile, 1966–1972*, published in 1978 by Arthur H. Stockwell Limited (Publishers) of Elms Court, Ilfracombe, Devon, United Kingdom.

Interestingly, the 1978 publication was deemed so useful by Africanists that Professor Anthony Kirk-Greene (1925–2018)—a Fellow of Saint Antony's College, Oxford, and president of the African Studies Association of the UK from 1988 to 1990—did a passionate review of it. We are, indeed, very grateful to Professor Kirk-Greene and several others, including our late beloved Oxford-educated Mwalimu (Professor) Ali A. Mazrui (1933–2014), who held an honorific Ghanaian title of *Nana*, and thanks to Professor Albert A. Adu Boahen (1932–2006), whose own writings on Ghana provided us with inspiration. We are, indeed, very grateful to all of the scholars, whose works have enabled us to complete a new biography of the late president Osagyefo Kwame Nkrumah of Ghana. Professor Kirk-Greene should have been happy to know that among our sources of inspiration in completing this book is his former Oxford student: Professor Olufemi ("Femi") Vaughan, currently the Alfred Sargent Lee '41 and Mary Ames Lee Professor of African Studies at Amherst College, Amherst, Massachusetts. Brother Femi (as we always call him) and his dear spouse (Sister Rosemary) deserve our thanks and appreciation; for Brother Femi, Professor Kirk-Greene is one of the three distinguished Africanists, who have influenced his scholarship; similarly, we are in Brother Fem's superb intellectual debt, including providing an endorsement for the book!!

Professor Samuel Zalanga of Bethel University is a distinguished classroom professor and also writer. Happily, he has always been in our corner in a variety of ways. For Yvette's "conspiracy" (with SIR Toyin) to surprise me with a major event, when I was honored as an Emeritus Professor at Indiana University, our Nigerian brother—with his generous spirit—was part of the inner "clique." He has also played a yeoman's role in what we discussed in chapter 3 of the book, as his superb knowledge of Pan-Africanism and its new interpretation were very beneficial to that chapter. In fact, we cannot thank him enough but, at least, we can let him know that we are eternally grateful to him, as Brother Samuel (as we call him) remains our gentle intellectual giant. We also thank Sister Ruth, his wonderful spouse, who is also a source of sisterly inspiration!

Above all, a distinguished University of London-educated historian, of Australian origin, Mrs. June Milne (1920–2018), deserves mention because "His Panaf Books," as post–1966 publishers of Nkrumah's works, helped us tremendously in coming across several useful sources for this book, including publications under its "Panaf Great Lives" series. Among them were short biographies of Nkrumah, Eduardo Mondlane, Patrice Lumumba, and Sekou Toure. Playing a role as a proofreader for Panaf Books between 1970 and 1972 enabled co-author Assensoh to come across very essential Nkrumah materials, which have assisted us in our own work. Very young Nkrumah scholars, whose published research also provided useful tips for this book include Dr. Ama Biney (formerly of School of Oriental and African Studies, SOAS) and Dr. Harcourt Fuller (formerly of London School of Economics). Both of them completed dissertations on several aspects of Nkrumah's life and, in the end, worked hard to revise them to be published. Co-author Assensoh was invited by Jamaican-born Dr. Fuller—at the time an Associate History Professor at Georgia State University in Atlanta, Georgia—to write a foreword to his 2014 Palgrave-Macmillan book, *Building the Ghanaian Nation-State: Kwame Nkrumah's Symbolic Nationalism*. We are grateful to both of them.

Acknowledgments

We are happy to point out that our interests to produce a publishable manuscript about four Ghanaian topical personalities—including the late president Nkrumah and the Cultural Prince, Dr. Kyerematen—did originate from our close friendship with University of Ghana's distinguished History Professor John K. (J.K.) Fynn (1935–2005) of Abura-Dunkwa Kona Royal Family in the Central Region of Ghana. Some very serious academic discussions with Dr. Fynn—a cousin of the Tsiboes, who owned Abura Printing Press, publishers of *The Pioneer* newspaper that co-author Assensoh served as Deputy Editor in early 1070s—gave us the impetus to think about writing fresh biographies of Nkrumah; publisher J.K. Tsiboe; Dr. Emmanuel James Kwegyir Aggrey; and Dr. Kyerematen, founder of the Ghana National Cultural Center in Kumasi, Ghana.

As the late Professor Fynn explained to us, at the time, the first silk (or flannel-like) suit that Nkrumah often wore as he traveled to serve as the general secretary of the nationalist group of the then Gold Coast (UGCC) and a small leather briefcase were bought for him by Mr. J.W. Tsiboe, his cousin. "Cousin J.W. Tsiboe wanted Nkrumah to look sharp in public," he said with his infectious laughter. Professor Fynn also did explain how Mrs. Nancy Tsiboe, his cousin's wife, was an insider of Nkrumah's political group, which later gained an upper hand in the nationalist struggle, thus leading to political victory for Nkrumah and his followers, referred to as the "verandah boys." Professor Fynn thought that the Tsiboes did so much for the future president of Ghana (Kwame Nkrumah) that the break in the UGCC leadership for Nkrumah to form his own Convention People's Party (CPP) was very unfortunate. Otherwise, Mr. Tsiboe, Mrs. Tsiboe, and Nkrumah would have instead remained in the same political camp in order for their publishing company—The Abura Printing Press of Adum, Kumasi—to benefit later from Nkrumah's government, especially in getting import licenses for ordering newsprint and other printing needs from overseas sources.

Dr. Fynn was, however, glad that their newspaper *The Pioneer* remained a very staunch supporter of the Busia-Danquah political coalition, which became the future political opposition to Nkrumah and his CPP Government. Since co-author A.B. Assensoh, in the early 1970s, worked for *The Pioneer*, we are very grateful to Dr. Fynn (as we called him always) for his encouragement and priceless information. The son, Mr. J.K. Tsiboe—a very gentle soul and very non-political—took over as managing director of the Press when his father (Mr. J. W. Tsiboe) passed away; he and Dr. Fynn were also very close. Professor Fynn, we are eternally grateful to you!

Pleasantly, former colleagues, who often checked to see the status of the book are Professor C.J. Wiltz of Baton Rouge, Rouge, Louisiana, and Emeritus History Professor Dorothy V. Smith of McComb, Mississippi. Our years at Dillard University, where Dr. Wiltz was our departmental chairperson, were fruitful. They have promised to own copies of this book when published; we believe them because they possess copies of *A Matter of Sharing* (2014) and *Migrant Stories* (2016), volumes 1 and 2 of A.B.'s published memoirs as well as our co-authored biographies, *Malcolm X: A Biography* (2014) and *Malcolm X and Africa* (2016).

Indeed, we are happy to point out the fact that we share mutual interests in the study of Nkrumah, Sekou Toure, and Pan-Africanism with Professor Emmanuel Kwaku Akyeampong of Harvard University, who is a distinguished scholar and author as well. Apart from being an ordained minister like A.B., we were happy to learn that he visited Conakry, the Guinean capital (just as A.B. did in the late 1960s), in his instance to complete his own research on the late president Sekou Toure and Nkrumah, and that he has also begun his own publishable work on a select number of postcolonial African leaders, including the late presidents Nkrumah and Toure (whose widow he met during the Conakry visit). Indeed, telephonic discussions with him are always very fruitful. When his work is published, we expect it to be very beneficial to researchers and students completing their own studies of Nkrumah and other Pan-African leaders. During a visit to Boston, co-author Alex-Assensoh (Yvette) and Kwadwo had a delightful dinner meeting with Professor Akyeampong as well as his scholar-spouse (Lady Ntuli, also of Harvard); son, Emmanuel (Junior); and young sister (Naledi).

Indeed, we happily acknowledge the prompt intellectual kindness of Professor Isidore Lobinbe of Southwest Oregon University, who invited us—as a former Fellow of South Africa's STIAS—to listen to a very illuminating lecture by Harvard University Endowed History Professor Emmanuel Akyeampong, a Fellow of STIAS, titled "Early Independent Africa's Abortive Attempt at Industrialization: The Case of Ghana under Kwame Nkrumah," the lecture refreshed several aspects of our memory of the work we have completed on Ghana's late president Nkrumah. Thank you very much, Brother Isidore!

Above all, we are again very grateful to our sons (Kwadwo Alex Stephen Assensoh and Livingston Alex Kwabena Assensoh) for their cooperation in a variety of ways, including helping with research and also looking for library sources for us as students of University of Oregon (from where Kwadwo, as an older brother, has graduated, with a major in Political Science, and a minor in Spanish). They often nudged us about the publishing date, as they are also intrigued about Ghana's late president Kwame Nkrumah, whose published 1957 autobiography they are very familiar with. We are again very grateful to Kwadwo ("K.") and Livingston (Livy).

Chronology of Kwame Nkrumah

IMPORTANT DATES AND TIMES IN HIS LIFE (1909–1972)

1909: His birth took place this year at Nkroful, Western Region of the Gold Coast (now Ghana), on September 21. Male children of Akan-speaking people, born on Saturdays, are usually named as Kwame, but his first name was changed from that of a Tuesday-born (i.e., Kwabena), hence Nkrumah's first name remained Kwame, although he was born on a Tuesday in that year. At his birth, Ghana was known as the Gold Coast due to the large deposits of gold being mined by colonial British mining companies. On March 6, 1957, the Gold Coast would be re-named Ghana at independence, with Nkrumah as the first elected indigenous leader, with the title of prime minister.

1914–1918: This is the period of World War I in which the United Kingdom (UK) and its allies were involved. The then Gold Coast and other colonial territories contributed troops to assist the British and ally troops. Most of the African troops saw military action in the former Burma, now re-named as Myanmar in Southeast Asia.

1920s–1934: Nkrumah, as a young adult, finished elementary school, entered Achimota College's teacher training program on a signed bond to teach for five years; upon graduation, he taught in elementary schools in Western Region of Ghana, mainly among his fellow Nzima ethnic (tribal) group. He also prepared to travel to America for further studies because of influences from America-educated Dr. James Emmanuel K. Aggrey of Achimota College and Nigeria-born Dr. Nnamdi Azikiwe, who introduced him specifically to Lincoln University in Pennsylvania, USA.

Figure C.1 Kwame Nkrumah. Photo taken circa 1935 by a campus photographer when Nkrumah was an undergraduate student at Lincoln University in Pennsylvania, USA.

1935: This year, in the summer, Nkrumah prepared and left by ship, from Takoradi Harbor, in Western Region of the then Gold Coast, for America for further studies. Nkrumah traveled through the Port of Liverpool, near London, stayed with Mr. & Mrs. Watson in their UK home. After obtaining his visa, he stayed in the United Kingdom for about two weeks and left on another boat for the United States. Upon arrival in New York, Nkrumah went to Oxford, Pennsylvania to enroll at the Lincoln University as a freshman; he disclosed that he had an equivalent of about $40 in his pocket, but the university officials generously allowed him to register and also helped him to have work-study arrangement in order for him to earn money for incidentals.

1939: At Lincoln University's commencement exercises, this year, Nkrumah was awarded his Bachelor of Arts (B.A.) degree with double majors in Sociology and Economics. To be able to stay in America, immigration rules expected him to be in school. Therefore, he enrolled in the Lincoln Theological Seminary to earn a Theology degree, whether he needed it or not.

1942: Nkrumah completed the studies to receive his Bachelor of Sacred Theology (B.S.T.) degree as the valedictorian of his graduation class, thereby being asked by the Dean of the Seminary to give the oration of the year. Nkrumah spoke on, "Abyssinia shall be free." This same year, he also earned a master's degree in Education from University of Pennsylvania.

1943–1945: Nkrumah, who had enrolled in graduate studies at University of Pennsylvania in both Education and Philosophy, was teaching as an Adjunct Instructor at Lincoln University. He earned a second master's degree in Philosophy and, in 1945, became an All-But-Dissertation (ABD) graduate student of University of Pennsylvania. After his part-time work in the cold weather, Nkrumah suffered from pneumonia. Subsequently, he felt unable to continue work on his dissertation, in June of this year, he left America for good to return to the Gold Coast, via London, UK. Nkrumah, assisted by Jomo Kenyatta of Kenya, served as co-secretary of the year's Pan-African Congress.

1946: Nkrumah, who had enrolled at Lincoln's Inn to study Law, also enrolled at London School of Economics (LSE) to study under Professor (Sir) Ayer, a British philosopher, for his doctorate (Ph.D.) He later abandoned the studies to work full time for much-needed funds. He worked full time for the West African Secretariat, where he and others assisted immigrants and new foreign students.

1947: In June, this year, Nkrumah and his future Foreign Minister Mr. Kojo Botsio left the United Kingdom for the Gold Coast by ship via Liverpool. On his way home, he stopped in Liberia and Sierra Leone. Nkrumah's shipping fare home from the United Kingdom was paid by Dr. J.B. Danquah, a London University-educated lawyer back in the Gold Coast so that he would serve as Secretary-General of the United Gold Coast Convention (UGCC), a semi-political and social group. Sadly, Dr. Danquah would end up in Nkrumah's political prison and, indeed, died there in the mid-1960s. Dr. Azikiwe criticized Nkrumah for that act.

1948–1949: By mid-1948, the UGCC leadership had come under suspicion by the British colonial officials. The leaders of the UGCC were also having disagreements with Nkrumah, who was suspected of being a Communist. After all of them ended up in colonial prisons, after which he broke with the leadership, which paid him 100 British Pounds Sterling a month. He subsequently formed his own Convention People's Party (CPP), which he ambitiously referred to as a party. Utilizing the non-violent tactics of India's Mahatma Gandhi, Nkrumah got his supporters and party members to go on strikes and to boycott British-made goods unless the Gold Coast was given its freedom. He named his tactics, positive action, and even published a pamphlet, titled "What I mean By Positive Action." All of these anti-British activities landed Nkrumah in jail for a non-felony conviction; his crime was sedition.

1950–1951: The British colonial authorities agreed to hold political elections for the indigenous parties, including the UGCC. Nkrumah was in jail but his colleagues of the CPP were campaigning for the party. In the end, when Nkrumah's CPP won the elections, the British freed him from prison to form a semi-autonomous government. Instead of prime minister, Nkrumah became Leader of Government Business. It was the same time that his *alma mater* (Lincoln University) invited and honored him with an honorary Doctor of Laws (LL.D) degree at the 1951 commencement, at which Nkrumah was the speaker. The then President Horace Mann Bond of Lincoln University was invited to visit the Gold Coast (future Ghana), and he accepted.

1957: After serving as Leader of Government Business, Nkrumah was informed that in this year, the Gold Coast would receive its independence from the British colonial leaders. As a leader of historicity, he and his allies agreed that the independence date should coincide with March 6, 1844, when the British formally began to rule the Gold Coast. There were to be elections for the future prime minister position, which Nkrumah and his CPP won. So, on March 6, 1957, Ghana became independent. President Bond, the late Rev. Dr. Martin Luther King, Jr. and his wife, Coretta, and several other civil rights leaders from the United States and Caribbean, including Jamaica's future prime minister Michael Manley, were among the invited dignitaries. The U.S. vice president Richard M. Nixon and his wife, Pat, represented President Dwight Eisenhower and the U.S. government; he met Dr. King for the first time at the Ghana event. This time, Nkrumah officially became the new Ghana's first elected indigenous leader.

1960: On July 1, Nkrumah, who won elections for the new presidential title, declared Ghana a republican nation, no longer accepting the Queen of the United Kingdom as its titular Head of State. President Nkrumah, this time, began an ambitious socialist agenda to the irritation or annoyance of his British-trained political opponents. Apart from socialist economists being invited to advise Nkrumah, the new president also accepted Caribbean-born Sir William Arthur Lewis to come to Ghana as an economic adviser.

1962: As President of Ghana, Nkrumah made an impromptu visit to Kumasi, the Ashanti regional capital, which played a decisive role in his electoral fortunes when he successfully campaigned to become the first elected president of the new Republic of Ghana in 1960. He was grateful to the reigning Asantehene, Nana Sir Otumfuo Osei Agyeman Prempeh II, and his sub-chiefs for the peaceful manner in which the Ashanti Region participated in the 1960 republican election. It was in Kumasi, at this time, that Nkrumah was introduced to Dr. A.A.Y. Kyerematen of the then Ashanti Cultural Center; Nkrumah agreed to support the center financially and, subsequently, its name was changed to the National Cultural Center of Ghana on his advice. The name change was to reflect a national character to satisfy Nkrumah's nationalistic fervor.

1965–1966: In 1965, Nkrumah, who had authored several books when in office as Ghana's leader, wrote the most controversial one titled *Neo-Colonialism: The Last Stage of Imperialism* in 1965. Reportedly, opposition leader Dr. K.A. Busia (1913–1978)–at the time in exile at the University of Oxford–drew the attention of American-elected Congressional leaders to the book. President Johnson's American government was also very angry about the book and, as John Stockwell wrote in *In Search of Enemies: A CIA Story* (1978), the CIA was authorized, at that point, to encourage anti-Nkrumah coup makers inside Ghana. That was why, when Nkrumah was on his way to Southeast Asia to mediate in the Vietnam War, his CPP government—with an open socialistic outlook and developmental program—was overthrown in a joint Ghana Army-Police-led *coup d'etat*, led by the assassinated General Emmanuel K. Kotoka (1926–1967), who successfully collaborated with other military and police officials. Formed in place of Nkrumah's regime was the National Liberation Council (NLC), headed by retired General Joseph Arthur Ankrah. Guinean President Sekou Toure welcomed deposed President Nkrumah as Guinea's co-president and provided him with political asylum.

1967: On April 17, General Kotoka was assassinated by forces led by Lieutenants S.B. Arthur and Moses Yeboah, both of the Ho-based Recce Squadron, in an unsuccessful counter-coup in Ghana which reportedly was meant to restore Nkrumah to power. Also killed were some younger military officers with him as security detail.

1968–1972: Deposed President Nkrumah continued to live in Guinea, since 1966, from where he authored several other books, including *Dark Days in Ghana*; *Challenge of the Congo*; *Axioms of Kwame Nkrumah*; *The Specter of Black Power*; and others. Several of these publications were issued or re-issued by Panaf Books of London, which was established by Mrs. June Milne to publish Nkrumah's post-1966 books, as several traditional Western publishers, in order not to offend the NLC regime, which replaced Nkrumah's CPP regime, refused to handle the deposed president's new book manuscripts. In fact, in 1969, Nkrumah's former political opponent (Oxford-educated Professor Kofi Abrefa Busia) was installed as post-NLC Ghana's prime minister with executive powers. The ceremonial president Edward Akufo-Addo, father of Ghana's current president, was one of the "Big Six" of the UGCC era.

In 1972, it became known that deposed President Nkrumah was in Bucharest, Romania, getting cancer treatment at a local clinic in the capital. When the executed General Ignatius Kutu Acheampong led a military coup to unseat Prime Minister Busia's Progress Party regime on January 13, 1972, Nkrumah was too ill to return to Ghana to play any role in the new government. He, in fact, died on Thursday, April 27, 1972 in Romania, and his body was later flown to Guinea for a large national celebratory honor, led by the then President Sekou Toure, before it was released to Ghana to be entombed in Accra, the capital; former Ghana First Lady Madam Fathia Nkrumah has been buried next to Dr. Nkrumah at the Kwame Nkrumah Memorial Park upon her death in Cairo, Egypt on May 31, 2007.

1974: Ghana's late president Kwame Nkrumah was among a select number of African Leaders, who were honored, this year, by the United Nations in New York for their sustained and relentless fight against apartheid South Africa. His UN gold medallion was received in New York, on his behalf, by his widow (Madam Fathia Nkrumah). The ruling National Redemption Council (NRC), which had overthrown Dr. Busia's Progress Party (PP) regime, sent its foreign Minister (Lt.-Colonel) Kwame Baah (1938–1997) to New York to support Mrs. Fathia Nkrumah and also to host a post-presentation reception for the occasion at the Ghana Mission to the UN.

1976: The founder and long-term Director of Ghana's National Cultural Center, Oxford University- and Cambridge University-educated Dr. A.A.Y. Kyerematen (1916—1976), who met Nkrumah and received help from him for his cultural center, died this year, and he was honored with a national funeral due to his respectable stature in the evolution of Ghana's high cultural image.

Chapter 1

Birth, Early Education, and Employment

Ghana's late president Kwame Nkrumah—dubbed Osagyefo by many of his admirers—was born in the then-Gold Coast (renamed Ghana on March 6, 1957). At the time of his birth in 1909, children's births were either recorded wrongly or not even recorded at all. That is why, in his published autobiography—titled *Ghana: Autobiography of Kwame Nkrumah* (Nelson, 1957)—he did speculate about his own birth and its exact date, settling for a date that coincided with a major ethnic event. Consequently, his birth was officially registered and observed as having occurred on Friday, September 21, 1909, in the small village of Nkroful in the Western Region.[1] However, his first name of Kwame, in Ghana's Akan linguistic idiom, meant that he was born on a Saturday.

Although it was known that Nkrumah was the only son of Madame Nyaniba, it was also a fact that Nkrumah was raised in a polygamous home for his father Nwia Kofi had several other children from his other wives. To support his family, young Nkrumah's father worked hard as the area's goldsmith.[2]

EARLY EDUCATION

Nkrumah attended the local Roman Catholic schools until Standard Seven, his final year of primary school. The school was run by Roman Catholic priests, and one of them, Father Fischer, is said to have taken a keen interest in Nkrumah. It was Fr. Fischer who recruited him as a Pupil Teacher for the local elementary (Junior and Senior) school. While in this position, Kwame Nkrumah took the national entrance examination and was admitted to Achimota's teacher training department. It was there that he first encountered Dr. James Emmanuel Kwegyir Aggrey (1875–1927), an official of the school, who died suddenly while visiting the United States, his wife's country of birth. Nkrumah wrote in his 1957 autobiography that Dr. Aggrey's death did pain him tremendously.[3]

In Nkrumah's published 1957 autobiography, *Ghana: Autobiography of Kwame Nkrumah*, he wrote the following about Dr. Aggrey:

> It was because of my great admiration for Aggrey, both as a man and a scholar, that I first formed the idea of furthering my studies in the United States of America. My plan was to finish the teacher-training course, return to teaching for five years and endeavor to save the necessary passage money.[4]

Preparation for American Education

When Nkrumah graduated from the teacher training section of Achimota College in 1930, he became a teacher at the Roman Catholic Junior High School at Elmina, in Western Ghana. It was from this job that he planned to save enough money to prepare for the United States where he would study hard like his mentor, Dr. Aggrey. Consequently, in 1935, after serving the requisite contract (bond), he applied for admission into Lincoln University, a historically Black university near Oxford, Pennsylvania, which was established as a private university in 1854, to offer college-level education to male Blacks; it became a public institution in 1972, and is noted as America's first degree-granting Historically Black College and University (HBCU).[5]

After receiving the relevant application materials from the dean of Admissions, Nkrumah promptly mailed back the completed forms to Lincoln University, and began studying the official bulletin, titled *Herald*, to be fully informed about the institution he hoped to be enrolled at. The fact that Lincoln University was a historically Black institution impressed him a lot.[6]

Although Dr. Aggrey was the initial impetus for Nkrumah's decision to study in America, Nnamdi Azikiwe of the Igbo ethnic group and first Nigerian president was the reason behind his application to Lincoln University, as the institution was Dr. Azikiwe's alma mater, as confirmed by Dr. Woeli Dekutsey:

> Following the encouragement of Dr. Azikiwe, Kwame Nkrumah applied to Lincoln University in the USA. When the good news came that he had secured admission, Kwame Nkrumah was still teaching at Amissano, not too far from Elmina. But, unfortunately for him, he did not have enough money to pay

his fare to America. He therefore decided to stow away on a ship at Takoradi harbor to travel to his uncle, H.K. Biney at Apapa wharf in Lagos, to seek his [financial] help.[7]

While Kwame Nkrumah was waiting for the Lincoln University admission, he left his first teaching post at the Catholic elementary school in Axim, by accepting a new teaching position at the Amissano Catholic Seminary, near Elmina, "where the [Catholic] church's indigenous clergy or priests were to be trained for the first time."[8] Nkrumah's trip to Nigeria was successful because he was able to hide in the boiler room of the ship, on which he had stowed away. Upon his arrival at the Nigerian harbor he managed to sneak out to meet Mr. Biney, his uncle, a very affluent businessman. Dr. Dekutsey explained in *Kwame Nkrumah: The Great African*, a slim 2012 book, that Nkrumah failed to apprise his uncle of his visit to Nigeria to seek financial assistance for America to further his education. His uncle was only able to give him partial monetary assistance, which necessitated supplementing his American trip with his savings, arriving there via the United Kingdom. In fact, "in those days, there were no American consular services in the Gold Coast, so everybody journeying to America had to travel first to the UK for an American visa."[9]

Upon Nkrumah's arrival in the United Kingdom, he stayed with a Gold Coast merchant in Liverpool, who was related to Pa Grant, himself a timber merchant in the country, who would later play a major role in the anti-colonial nationalist liberation movement, from which Nkrumah would eventually benefit. It was when in Liverpool that Nkrumah read from the British newspapers that Mussolini's Italy had invaded Ethiopia and the young emperor Haile Selassie had been exiled. The news angered Nkrumah and, as he later made known, the news about Ethiopia—sometimes called Abyssinia by Pan-Africanists—also did make "my nationalism [surge] to the fore."[10] It was an episode which among other reasons prompted Nkrumah to seek higher education in America and return home to save his country and other colonies from what he saw as the clutches of colonialism.[11]

NOTES

1. Ibid., p. 1.
2. Ibid., p. 1.
3. Kwame Nkrumah. 1957. *Ghana: The Autobiography*. London: Thomas Nelson & Sons, Publishers.
4. Kwame Nkrumah. 1971. *Ghana: Autobiography of Kwame Nkrumah*. New York: International Publishers, p. 15.

5. A.B. Assensoh. 1989. *Kwame Nkrumah of Africa.* Ilfracombe, UK: Arthur H. Stockwell Publishers, p. 43.

6. Nkrumah, op. cit., p.15.

7. Woeli Dekutsey. 2012. *Kwame Nkrumah: The Great African.* Accra: Woeli Publishing Services, p. 5.

8. Assensoh, 1989, op. cit., p. 44.

9. Dekutsey, 2012, op. cit., p. 5.

10. Ibid., p. 5.

11. Ibid., p. 6.

Chapter 2

Overseas Student Years

Nkrumah's American and UK Sojourns, 1935–1947

As stated earlier, it was at Government Teacher Training College—which was part of Achimota College, near Accra—that the future Ghanaian president Kwame Nkrumah nurtured the idea of traveling to the United States in search of higher education, the proverbial golden fleece. Again, the impetus for that interest stemmed from Nkrumah's meeting with the assistant principal, late Dr. James Emmanuel Kwegyir (J.E.K.) Aggrey, who had studied in America, and had made a positive impression on the young man during his freshman year as the assistant vice-principal of the college. The fact that Aggrey was the first African member of staff of the college, whose serving staff was generally made up of White employees greatly influenced the attitude of the future Pan-Africanist.

With the influences of Aggrey and Nigeria's Dr. Nnamdi Azikiwe, Nkrumah decided to travel to America for further postgraduate studies. After the strenuous preparations, Nkrumah received much-needed help from some family members, including a merchant at Apapa, near Lagos, Nigeria. Nkrumah was very glad that at last the opportunity had come for him to leave, yet he found it hard to leave his mother by herself to study in America. He, among other details, wrote: "My joy [of leaving] was shadowed. However, by the thought of having to break the news to my mother. I knew how much I meant to her and how deeply she would grieve over my going [to America]."[1]

To pacify his mother, Nkrumah decided to travel home to stay with her for several days until the night he was to leave the Gold Coast. The mother, Madam Nyanibah, was duly informed and, as Nkrumah has indicated in his published memoir, *Ghana: Autobiography of Kwame Nkrumah*, the mother showed no emotion. Instead, she and Nkrumah had very meaningful discussions until the following morning. According to Nkrumah, the mother also told him "of my claim to two stools of chieftaincies in the country, including those of Nsaeum in Wasaw Efiase and Dadieso in Aowin area of the Western region of the country." It simply meant that if Nkrumah decided to not leave for America, then one day he could be enstooled as an important chief.[2]

All of the foregoing preparations were in 1935. After staying with his mother for about a week to reveal to her his intentions, he woke up one morning to pack his personal belongings to depart for the Port of Takoradi, from where he was to board a ship for the Port of Liverpool in the United Kingdom on his way to America, where he had been admitted to study at Lincoln University. In fact, Bankole Timothy, his Sierra Leonean biographer, described it best in the following words:

> Kwame Nkrumah's dream came true in August [of] 1935 when he was nearly twenty-six [years old]. With the help of relatives and friends, he sailed for the United States of America from the port of Takoradi via Liverpool. Thus, began the search of Kwame Nkrumah for higher education.[3]

NKRUMAH'S ARRIVAL IN AMERICA

According to young Nkrumah, in his search for higher education in America, he did not want to stay too long in the United Kingdom. After all, he was very serious about getting more education to return to the then-Gold Coast to help his country. Therefore, as he wrote in his 1957 published memoir, he stayed in the port city of Liverpool for only two weeks. However, while staying with a relative in Liverpool, he recalled a feminist incident that surprised him. According to the future leader of Ghana in his memoir he was having a meal with the host and his wife. Suddenly, in response to something the host said, his wife shot back saying to her husband, "Oh, don't be silly."[4] Recalling that in African traditional society, many men, at the time, expected women to be subservient, Nkrumah expected his host would rebuke his wife for her sharp retort so he "waited, anxious and embarrassed, for the man's rebuke. But he took not the slightest offence and carried on talking."[5] That, indeed, was a good lesson for the young Nkrumah as it prepared him well for the Western society in which he was getting ready to be involved as a student in America.

After the lesson Nkrumah had learned about marital relationship, he wrote that he boarded one of the ships owned by the Cunard White Star Line, a shipping company. Compared to his trip from the Gold Coast to the United Kingdom, Nkrumah wrote, "This trip was very much better than my previous one from Takoradi to Liverpool because I made several friends. One of them, a young Dutchman, who was going out to finish his theological program at

Harvard Divinity School, remained a good friend of mine the whole time that he was in America."[6]

Upon his arrival in New York, Nkrumah found his way to Pennsylvania and arrived at Lincoln University, which had admitted him as an undergraduate student with a small scholarship. However, upon his arrival on the campus in late 1935, he had with him only an equivalent of 80 American dollars and, as a result, displeased the university officials. At that point, Nkrumah agreed to accept part-time campus jobs to augment the little money that he had. At the time, among the jobs available to him was one at the University Library, where he helped in shelving books, while enrolling for his studies.[7] As Nkrumah explained later in life, the choice of working at the Lincoln University Library was not his to make. He explained:

> There were two opportunities of earning money, which were open to scholarship holders. We could act as library assistants and also wait in dining hall. As it happened, the work in the library was a great pleasure to me but, in any case, there was no job, however distasteful, that I would not have attempted at that time [to make money].[8]

Despite the library job, Nkrumah knew that his limited academic scholarship required that he studied hard and, as a result, he vowed to excel in all of his classes in the double academic majors of economics and sociology with a scheduled commencement of 1939. What helped the young Nkrumah at the time was the decision of his two professors in sociology and economics to give the classes several private readings requiring simply that students submit reports. Apart from doing his own reports, Nkrumah did agree to assist classmates, who complained about these readings as he was "on the look out to line my [his] pockets."[9]

Over the years, as a student at Lincoln University, young Nkrumah learned how to survive financially and socially. That was why he got involved in public speech-making for which he was once placed second. He disclosed that he won a gold medal later in his life, but a girl he knew took it from him and kept it as a souvenir. It seemed that he was not disturbed by the girl's action because Nkrumah felt bad that he had very little time to spend with her. Socially, Nkrumah knew that he could increase his circle of friendship when he decided, as an upperclassman, to pledge to become a member of the Phi Beta Sigma Fraternity, which had a motto that he much admired "Culture for Service and Service for Humanity." Interestingly, Nkrumah disclosed, "Another girl relieved me of my Frat Pin."[10] Also, he socially prepared and got inducted into membership of the Prince Hall Freemasons in the thirty-second degree. As he said later, the motto of the organization—"To be one, ask one"—fascinated him as well.[11]

Chapter 2

PREPARATION TOWARD GRADUATION FROM LINCOLN UNIVERSITY

For Nkrumah to be allowed to pledge and become a fraternity member, it meant that he was doing well academically. Although his double majors were economics and sociology, the young Nkrumah took the opportunity to read widely and, in the process, studied philosophy, theology, anthropology, and other related subjects in the arts. It was, therefore, not surprising that his professors considered him to be a hard-working international student.[12]

Nkrumah had many plans for further studies upon his graduation from Lincoln University, an event that was fast approaching. For example, he wanted to become a professional journalist so he had plans to enter Columbia University, a plan that had to be shelved. This was because Nkrumah owed Lincoln University therefore was not given a transcript to apply to Columbia University to study Journalism at the graduate level. To raise funds, he instead agreed to work for the University's Theological Seminary as an assistant lecturer in philosophy in 1939. As he could enroll in a local university without a problem, Nkrumah started graduate studies in philosophy at the University of Pennsylvania, which he finished a year later and enrolled in the doctoral (PhD) program in that subject. He had earlier enrolled in the Seminary at Lincoln. In 1945, ambitious Nkrumah completed the course work for the doctoral degree. With a scholarship of 100 dollars from the Presbyterian Church, he was able to afford books for his classes. Luckily for him, in 1942, Nkrumah completed the theology degree, at the head of his graduating class, so was chosen to give the oration for the year's graduation, thus showing how serious he was about his studies.[13]

NKRUMAH'S ARGUMENT WITH HIS SEMINARY DEAN

While a student at Achimota College, Nkrumah was tremendously influenced by Dr. James Emmanuel K. Aggrey, who died in the United States during a sabbatical leave. After his death, the Columbia University–educated Aggrey was buried in Salisbury, North Carolina, where his wife and children lived. So, while lecturing at the Lincoln Theological Seminary, Nkrumah and several African students decided to travel to Salisbury to visit the grave of Dr. Aggrey. The actions of Nkrumah and his colleagues did get back to Dr. Johnson, Dean of the Seminary.

It was reported that instead of Nkrumah and his colleagues offering prayers for the deceased Aggrey, they chose to do it the African traditional way by pouring libation, invoking the gods of Africa to protect and help Aggrey. Dean Johnson, to say the least, was very enraged by the pagan manner in which Nkrumah, his former Seminary student and, now, a lecturer on campus, had behaved. The Dean, as confirmed by available Lincoln University records and newspaper accounts, wrote a lengthy letter to Nkrumah in which he complained bitterly about the un-Christian way he acted on the grave of Dr. Aggrey, a man of letters and a Christian. Unfortunately, Nkrumah too felt offended by the Dean's characterization of the ceremony on Aggrey's grave as being ungodly. What incensed Dean Johnson again was his awareness that Nkrumah had been licensed by the Presbyterian Church in Chester to serve as an occasional preacher. In his brief and courteous response to Dean Johnson, Nkrumah simply explained that, in fact, all he and his colleagues did in Salisbury was to act traditionally and customarily as Africans. That was the end of the matter.[14]

NKRUMAH'S STUDENT ACTIVISM IN AMERICA

The area, through which Nkrumah got to know several other students from Africa, was in his years as university student activist in the United States and, later in the United Kingdom. According to the available facts, as a student at Lincoln University, Nkrumah was contacted by two African students from Sierra Leone and Nigeria: future Sierra Leonean foreign minister John Karefa-Smart, a student at Otterbein College (now university) in Ohio and Prince A.A.N. Orizu of Nigeria, who was a student at Ohio State University in Columbus, Ohio. They informed Nkrumah of a new student organization they were forming in the early 1940s for African students in the United States and Canada. Eventually, there was an organizational meeting in New York during which Nkrumah was elected as the association's first president. That was done because he volunteered his name for the position.[15]

Also, since charity begins at home, Nkrumah and other students from the Gold Coast in Pennsylvania decided to form their own African students' association. These students included the foreign minister in Nkrumah's government Ako Adjei and Professor Jones Quartey, a former professor of extra-mural studies at the University of Ghana. Nkrumah wrote about how he "arranged for the publication of the Association's official newspaper, which was called the *African Interpreter.* Through the medium of this newspaper, we tried to revive a spirit of nationalism."[16]

Apart from the students from the Gold Coast in the association, there were also Nigerians. Nkrumah reported that there were continuous disagreements with the Nigerian students during their meetings. He couched these disagreements in the following words:

The Nigerians claimed that there was no question of considering African or West African unity at the existing stage of colonial dependency and insisted that we should leave these colonial territories to struggle for themselves, each one working out its own salvation at best it could, without any link or cooperation with the other territories. I and the Gold Coast students, on the other hand, felt strongly that the question of territorial solidarity—that is to say, each territory mapping out and planning its own liberation—could not hope for ultimate success until it was linked up with the other movements in West Africa.[17]

Very interestingly, these contentious issues with his Nigerian colleagues marked the beginning of Nkrumah's strong Pan-Africanist views. He had shown streaks of his Pan-Africanist nature very early in his life. For example, during meetings of the student organization as far back as the early 1940s, Nkrumah and his fellow students from the then Gold Coast stressed their belief in the fact that unless territorial freedom was "ultimately linked up with the Pan-African movement for the liberation of the whole African continent, there would be no hope of freedom and equality for the African and for the people of African descent in any part of the world."[18]

While serving as the president of Ghana, Dr. Kwame Nkrumah started to show disinterestedness in regional groupings as he felt that it could slow continental unity. However, as a student back in the United States, he strongly supported the idea of West African unity. As he had indicated in his published autobiography, the idea of West African unity "became the accepted philosophy of the African Students' Association and we directed the students that when they returned to their respective territories, they should work hard politically to organize particular areas, but that in so doing they should maintain close contact with the political activities of their territories."[19]

In fact, it became evident later on in the meetings of the erstwhile Organization for African Unity (OAU)—now the African Union (AU)—that the difference Nkrumah had with his Tanzanian colleague, the late president Julius K. Nyerere, was the fact that the East African leader and others in the sub-region believed in regional groupings, the reason behind the East African Federation, which had socio-economic links among all of the East African countries. At the time, Nkrumah had forgotten that, during his years as a student leader in America, he wanted other African student leaders as well as other members of his association to believe in West African unity, adding: "By this means, they would maintain not only unity within their own territories, but would pave the way for unity among all the territories in West Africa."[20]

NKRUMAH LEAVES AMERICA FOR GOOD

Apart from teaching pure Philosophy, Nkrumah was later promoted as a full-fledged lecturer at Lincoln University's Theological Seminary to teach elementary (first year) Greek as well as Social Philosophy and what was known at the time as Negro History. Nkrumah's teaching was much appreciated by his Lincoln University students that, as he confirmed, in the year that he decided to leave America for good, he received the honor by the campus magazine, *The Lincolnian*, as "the most outstanding professor of the year."[21]

Nkrumah, who arrived in America in 1935 as a student from the British colony of the Gold Coast, had lived and studied in America for a decade. In his final year in America, Nkrumah took a job from the Sun Shipbuilding Yard at Chester in Pennsylvania, serving as a counter; his eight-hour work schedule was from 12:00 a.m. midnight to 8:00 a.m. As Nkrumah put it, he got the job "in order to put body and soul together."[22]

Instead of actually keeping his body and soul together, Nkrumah seemed to have injured his body, for one morning, it felt too cold for Nkrumah, as he describes it in these words, "It froze so hard on several occasions that my hands almost stuck to the steel and although put on all the cloths that I possessed, I was chilled to the marrow."[23]

The chilly weather resulted in a diagnosis of pneumonia. This caused his decision to not only resign from the job but above all, to leave America. This is how he reported the incident after the physician of the shipbuilding company examined him and took his temperature:

> He immediately summoned the [company] ambulance and rushed me off to Chester hospital, where I was put into an oxygen tent, supposedly a critical condition. Coupled with this, probably because I realized how close I had been to death, I longed to see my mother again more than anything else in the world. By the time I was able to get out of bed, I had made up my mind that I would leave America and return home as soon as ever this could be arranged.[24]

It was, in fact in May 1945 that Nkrumah left New York for London, the first leg of his plans to return to the Gold Coast, where he could see his beloved mother. His friends made his departure memorable:

> Several of my friends came to wave me off at the quay side. I couldn't believe I was really leaving them, and that I was leaving the country that had been my home for ten years. I was too stunned for emotions to play much part in the leave-taking and it was not until the boat sailed out from the harbor, and I saw the Statue of Liberty with her arm raised as if in a personal farewell to me that a mist covered my eyes. "You have opened my eyes to the true meaning of liberty, I thought. I shall never rest until I have carried your message to Africa."[25]

Kwame Nkrumah, the student from a small town in the Gold Coast called Nkroful, had decided to leave America after 10 solid years of studying and struggling to survive on limited resources. He was on his way to London, and whether or not he would leave for the Gold Coast to see his beloved mother (Madam Nyanibah) was another matter.[26]

NKRUMAH'S EARLY OBSESSION WITH ETHIOPIA (AS ABYSSINIA)

Present-day Ethiopia was once known as Abyssinia but—between 4,000 and 2,000 BCE—the country, as it exists today, was known as the Kingdom of Punt. However, the Cushitic Kingdom of Damont, as northern Ethiopia was known, was said to have been established in 2,000 BCE.[27] It was, therefore, understandable when Nkrumah, as early as August 1935, had his nationalism agitated on a London street when he read a British newspaper headline: "Mussolini Invades Ethiopia." He confessed in his published 1972 autobiography: "That was all I needed. At that moment it was almost as if the whole of London had suddenly declared war on me personally."[28]

At the same time, Nkrumah knew that he was not ready to go and join forces with Ethiopian soldiers to fight Mussolini's Italy. However, as he continued to lament after seeing that headline, he commented his belief in nationalism: "My nationalism surged to the fore; I was ready and willing to go through hell itself, if need be, in order to achieve my object."[29]

Most certainly, Nkrumah's objective was to acquire higher education in the United States, as he did eventually, and return to Africa to confront the twin evils of colonialism and imperialism. However, he did not forget about Ethiopia, which some radical Africans referred to as Abyssinia. The fact that Nkrumah did not erase Ethiopia from his memory did show clearly in 1942 when he was graduating from the Lincoln Theological Seminary at the top of his class. He wrote about the incident in the following words:

> I graduated from the seminary at Lincoln with a Bachelor of Theology degree in 1942 at the head of my class. As [it] was the custom, the duty fell to me to deliver the seminary graduation oration that year. The subject I chose was "Ethiopia shall stretch forth her hands unto God . . ." It was a delivered extempore, and I was a little dubious as to its success. However, when professors and past students rushed forward to at the end to shake my hand enthusiastically, I knew that they had appreciated it.[30]

As it was the case with Nkrumah at the time, his Pan-Africanism was at its highest; hence, he was very incensed by the Ethiopian issue. Interesting, too, in the same period, around 1942, Ethiopia and Britain had resumed what was known as British-Ethiopia Frontier Politics of 1942–1948. The measure expected Ethiopia to re-assert her authority, while the British drove away the Italians from power and restored Ethiopian rule.³¹

As the elected leader of Ghana, Nkrumah's respect for Ethiopia, as an ancient kingdom, was demonstrated by the fact that he was always ready to visit its capital to attend OAU Annual Heads of State meetings, often with Emperor Haile Selassie playing active roles as the royal host. It was, indeed, not surprising that Nkrumah and his fellow African leaders, in May 1963, succeeded in founding the OAU, which as stated earlier is now called the AU. While Ghana's Kwame Nkrumah was deposed in a military coup in February 1966 and died in April 1972, Emperor Haile Selassie (1892–1975) suffered a similar fate in 1974, subsequently dying the following year, 1975.³²

NKRUMAH'S LONDON ACTIVISM AND SUBSEQUENT EVENTS

When Nkrumah arrived in the British capital of London in 1945, he had many plans. His most important desire upon embarking from New York's harbor was to return home to see his mother Madam Nyaneba. However, with several plans popping out of Nkrumah's busy head, the soon-to-be first elected indigenous Ghanaian Head of State had to shelve the idea of immediately returning to the Gold Coast. Why? He found himself in the midst of like-minded individuals. He made sure that he became friends with a West Indian agitator for Pan-Africanism, George Padmore, who was originally from Trinidad and Tobago. Nkrumah confirmed that in the following words:

> The only person I knew of in England was George Padmore, a West Indian Journalist, who lived in London and was the author of articles, which had aroused my interest and sympathy I was so impressed by his writings that I wrote a letter to him from the States introducing myself and asking whether he would be able to meet me at Euston [Train] Station when I arrived.³³

With help from Padmore and a few other Black residents of the former colonial capital, Nkrumah settled down and started to implement several of his ideas, which had brought him to the United Kingdom. For example, instead of traveling home to the Gold Coast, he changed plans in order to stay in the United Kingdom for two more years, in spite of the future Ghanaian president's ardent desire to put to fruitful use the knowledge he had acquired during his decade-long sojourn in the United States.³⁴

When he decided to remain in the United Kingdom, Nkrumah sought further studies, at least to complete his doctoral work in philosophy interrupted by his departure from the United States. However, some of his Lincoln

University contemporaries, including his future cabinet member, Ako Adjei, offered him advice with respect to what to study; studying law was one of the options. He confirmed, therefore, that upon his arrival in the capital, London, he did not waste any time in enrolling at Gray's Inn and, as required, started to attend lectures at the London School of Economics, where he came in direct contact with Professor Laski, who taught political science.[35] It became apparent that his subsequent meeting with George Padmore, dubbed Father of Pan-Africanism, was a strong reason prompting him to revise his plans. It was Padmore who fortunately who took him to the West African National Secretariat on Gray's Inn Road. There, Padmore introduced Nkrumah to several other Pan-Africanists and nationalists, several of whom were from South Africa, Sierra Leone, and Ethiopia.[36]

When Nkrumah left America in May 1945 for the United Kingdom, he still had the interest to continue his student activism, which he had started in earnest. That was why it should not have been surprising that the friend he knew well in London was George Padmore, the Trinidadian, who was not only the leading apostle of Pan-Africanism but also a practicing journalist. He was, therefore, excited that Padmore would take him first and foremost to the West African Students' Union Hostel, where he arranged and got a room. However, he did not like the formal atmosphere there, so decided to find new accommodations. He eventually visited the Tufnell Park area of London where he rented a room from an old lady for 30 British shillings a week, but without meals. However, he found the family to be very kind to him, as the mother always left food in the oven for him. Nkrumah happily wrote: "And this little room became my home for the whole of my state in London from June 1945 until November 1947."[37]

What Nkrumah did was different from his activities back in America as a student leader. For example, he initially joined the West African Students' Union in London, and very quickly became the vice president. Immediately after he joined the union, its focus was revised, as it started to assist new students with institutional registration as well as searching for accommodations for new arrivals. Also, Nkrumah and other students became involved in "agitating for better conditions in West Africa by petitions to the Colonial Office."[38] Nkrumah was delighted that he and his fellow student union leaders were able to assist other students in need. For example, some of the direct assistance included the fact that whenever students faced financial hardships, Nkrumah and the other leaders communicated with their families back home to request financial assistance for them. Very importantly, in emergency situations, Nkrumah and his student union colleagues did "endeavor to find a means of helping them out from its meager funds."[39]

Most certainly, Nkrumah seemed to find great delight in assisting other African students with their problems in London. For example, he got involved in helping other students in settling their disputes with their rental agencies, landlords, and land ladies. He, in fact, disclosed further: "Occasionally, someone would end in trouble with a girl [he] picked up in Piccadilly or the Tottenham Court road. Here was never a dull moment and I thoroughly enjoyed the work."[40] It was shortly after his arrival in London that Nkrumah started plans, with others, to organize the major Pan-African Congress. In the words of the late Kenya-born Professor Ali A. Mazrui, Nkrumah's arrival in the United Kingdom also had a tactical undertone, whereby he had plans to test out some of what he studied back in America. Dr. Mazrui added that, indeed, Nkrumah's initial serious experience of testing his organizational skills took place in London, as he was astutely involved with Kenya's Jomo Kenyatta in organizing the fifth Pan-African Congress in Manchester, shortly after his arrival from America. To keep busy and also earn money for his keep, Nkrumah's overall daily activities included accepting the position of secretary for the Secretariat, while organizing meetings as well as working very hard for the Colored Workers' Association of Great Britain. He also made plans for the publishing of a new nationalist newspaper, to be named *The New African*.[41]

Nkrumah and the other planners of the fifth Pan-African Congress were of the opinion that the four previous Congresses were monopolized by non-radical Africans, including middle-class and reactionary intellectuals. The future Ghanaian leader decided to be actively involved to see a different outcome. In the end, such planners as Dr. W.E.B. DuBois of the United States, Kenya's Jomo Kenyatta, Trinidad and Tobago's George Padmore, and Nkrumah himself made sure that among the invited participants were leaders of various cooperatives as well as trade unionists and student groups.[42] It was easily agreed that nationalism should be the theme for the fifth Pan-African Congress in Manchester. The planners further agreed to utilize the definition of nationalism as espoused and defined by Chatham House of London in a report; it was defined as a consciousness on the part of individuals or a group as well as a desire to allow to spearhead the strength, prosperity, or liberty of a nation.[43]

Unfortunately, not everything that Nkrumah sought to achieve at the time materialized. For example, as his biographers have pointed out, some of the organizations he associated with were not as progressive as he had hoped. Sadly, some of these organizations, which outwardly seemed progressive, were not. Some of them were indeed a great disappointment to him. Being very close to his country's colonial masters, the British, he felt very strongly that "the solution for the colonial subject peoples lay in their own hands and would be solved by their efforts."[44] While in London, Nkrumah had the time to implement all sorts of ideas that he had studied in college; for example, he experimented with such Leninist ideas as the formation of a group known as the "Circle," which discussed Marxist and Leninist ideas. Nkrumah used the organization to place emphasis on the importance of organization as well as the necessity of an African union. It was at that time he thought of united West Africa as an initial step toward the unification of the entire continent.[45]

One would notice that it became apparent that the future leader of Ghana (Nkrumah) was using his stay in the United Kingdom as a stepping-stone toward a mobilization of Africa's future leaders, including those from French-speaking West Africa, some of whom were already serving in the French Parliament as Deputies. Among those he met in France were the late Souros Apithy of the Republic of Dahomey (now Benin), Leopold Sedar Senghor of Senegal, Felix Houphouet-Boigny of the Ivory Coast, and others.[46] Indeed, Nkrumah's relationships, forged with several future African leaders while as students, helped him to persuade several of them later into forming the OAU in Ethiopia in 1963. Today, it has been renamed as the AU, which is still headquartered in Addis Ababa, the Ethiopian capital.

At the time, Nkrumah also forged ties between continental Africans and diasporan Blacks, which was aimed at bringing about rapid student exchanges, an encouragement of a serious study of Africans inhabiting the second largest continent in the world by overseas-based descendants of Africans. It also helped African Americans and Caribbean-based Blacks to put in place curricula that would enable diaspora Blacks in the Caribbean and North America study African history. Therefore, the 1945 Congress was deemed a great success.[47]

NKRUMAH'S PREPARATION FOR GOLD COAST POLITICS

According to Nkrumah, his plans to return from the United Kingdom to the then-Gold Coast came close to fruition when he received a letter from Ako Adjei, his contemporary at Lincoln University. According to Nkrumah, Ako Adjei asked him if he would return to serve as general secretary of the United Gold Coast Convention (UGCC). Nkrumah further added:

> He [Ako Adjei] explained that the U.G.C.C. was being faced with the problem of how to reconcile the leadership of the intelligentsia with the broad masses of the people and, knowing of my political activities in both the United States and in England, he had re-commended to the Executive Committee that I should be invited to become the general secretary. He added that the Executive Committee had offered to pay me one hundred pounds a month and to provide me with a car.[48]

That was in 1947, about two years after Nkrumah's arrival in the United Kingdom. Upon the perusal of the letter from Ako Adjei, Nkrumah was happy but, as he later explained, the offer from the UGCC simply seemed too good to be true; hence, he felt that "it might be better to be a little cautious and to try and find out more about what was going on in the Gold Coast."⁴⁹ As proof of his unease about the UGCC offer through Ako Adjei's correspondence, Nkrumah did his best to do his own investigations about the organization as well as the happenings in the Gold Coast, which was still under British colonial rule. At the time of his correspondence with Ako Adjei, Nkrumah was preparing for a West African National Conference that never materialized. The conference preparation was one of the reasons he was somewhat hesitant to make any hasty decision about returning to the Gold Coast to work for the UGCC.

Nkrumah's pondering over the possibility of accepting the UGCC offer coincided with his service with the West African Secretariat. He teamed up with Sierra Leone–born journalist by the name of I.T.A. Johnson to co-author a signed resolution in their capacities as secretary-general and chairman, respectively, of the Secretariat with the simple title: "A Resolution on Imperialists' Colonial Policy." Both African writers unreservedly condemned the obvious style by the colonialist to divide and conquer the African continent in a variety of ways, especially the nuance of dividing the world into advanced and the Third World. Robert K. Gardinera, Ghanaian who later became the first Executive Director of the Executive Commission for Africa (ECA) based in Addis Ababa Ethiopia, endorsed the statement as the executive secretary of the London-based Secretariat.⁵⁰

OTHER OBSERVATIONS ABOUT NKRUMAH IN LONDON

Nkrumah showed the funny side of his life upon arrival in London. Indeed, he narrated how, at a tube station, he decided to buy a newspaper during World War II period from a newspaper vendor, for everything seemed to be rationed. He, *inter alia*, wrote:

> I went to a newsboy and handed him the penny or two-pence, whatever the price was, and he told me to help myself. I picked up what I took to be a single copy, and as I was walking away the boy started running madly after me shouting: "Hi, there! Stop! I looked round wondering whatever could be wrong with him. Then, examining my purchase, I discovered that I had taken about ten copies of the newspaper by mistake. I had been so used to the bulky American papers that I never gave it a thought. I had forgotten the restriction of newsprint in England since the war. I explained this to the boy but I don't suppose he could believe it as he had probably never set eyes on any daily paper boasting of more than ten or twelve pages."⁵¹

Nkrumah found London very user friendly, as reflected in his comments. He liked, for example, the fact that there was freedom of movement and speech, something his future political opponents claimed he denied them during his leadership in Ghana. What fascinated Nkrumah was that nobody bothered about what others were doing, and there was nothing to stop him from getting on his feet and denouncing the whole of the colonial British Empire.

NOTES

1. Nkrumah, 1957, p. 25.
2. Ibid., p. 25.
3. Bankole Timothy. 1974. *Kwame Nkrumah: The Man Who Brought Independence to Ghana*. London, UK: Longman Group Limited (Publishers), pp. 5–6.
4. Ibid. p. 27.
5. Ibid., p. 27.
6. Ibid., p. 28.
7. Assensoh, 1989, pp. 5–52.
8. Nkrumah, op. cit., p. 30.
9. Ibid., p. 30.
10. Ibid., p. 31.
11. Ibid., p. 52.
12. Assensoh, 1989; op. cit., p. 51; Nkrumah, p. 20.
13. Nkrumah, op. cit., pp. 31–32; Assensoh, 1989, pp. 52–53.
14. Assensoh, 1989, op. cit., pp. 54–55.
15. Ibid., pp. 240–241.
16. Nkrumah, 1972, op. cit., p. 43.
17. Ibid., pp. 43–44..
18. Ibid., p. 44.
19. Ibid., p. 44.
20. Ibid., p. 44.
21. Ibid., pp. 32–33.
22. Ibid., p. 33.
23. Nkrumah, 1972, op. cit., p. 33.
24. Ibid., pp. 33–34.
25. Ibid., p. 49.
26. Bankole Timothy. 1974. *Kwame Nkrumah: The Man Who Brought Independence to Ghana*. London: Longmans' Publishers, 2. Here, the name of Nkrumah's mother is spelled as Nyanibah, instead of the past or earlier spelling, Madam Nyaneba.
27. Paulos Milkias. 2016. "Ethiopia." In *Africa: An Encyclopedia of Culture and Society*, edited by Toyin Falola & Daniel Jean-Jacques, 455. Santa Barbara/Denver, CO: ABC-CLIO.
28. Kwame Nkrumah, 1972, op. cit., p. 27.

29. Ibid, p. 27.
30. Ibid., p. 32.
31. Gufu Oba. 2013. *Nomads in the Shadows of Empires*. Leiden, The Netherlands & Boston, MA: Brill Academic Press (Publishers), p. 231.
32. Jeffrey S. Ahlman. 2021. *Kwame Nkrumah: Vision of Liberation*. Oxford, OH: Ohio University Press, pp. 24–25.
33. Ibid., 1974, op. cit., p. 2.
34. Ibid., p. 8.
35. Ibid., p. 8; Nkrumah's autobiography, op. cit., p. 51.
36. Ibid., pp. 8–9.
37. Ibid., p. 51.
38. Ibid., pp. 51–52.
39. Ibid., p. 52.
40. Ibid., p. 53.
41. Ali A. Mazrui. 1967. *On Heroes and Uhuru-Worship*. London: Longmans Publishers, pp. 114–115.
42. Thomas Hodgkin. 1957. *Nationalism In Colonial Africa*. New York: New York University Press, pp. 146–147.
43. Ibid., p. 20.
44. Panaf Publishers. 1974. *Kwame Nkrumah: A Biography*. London: Panaf Books Ltd., p. 33.
45. Kwame Nkrumah. 1973. *Revolutionary Path*. London: Panaf Books Ltd., p. 47.
46. Mazrui, op. cit., p. 115.
47. S.K.B. Asante. 1983. "Politics of Confrontation" (Part I) in *West Africa Magazine*, London, 10 January, p. 142.
48. Nkrumah, 1972, op. cit., p. 611.
49. Ibid., p. 61.
50. Robert Gardiner, "Wasu," in *The African Interpreter* (April, 47), p. 9; and Nkrumah's autobiography, pp. 56–57.
51. Ibid., p. 48.

Chapter 3

Kwame Nkrumah and Pan-Africanism: A New Interpretation

The independence of Ghana is meaningless unless it is linked [up] with the total liberation of the African continent.[1]

The late president Kwame Nkrumah (1909–1972) was Ghana's first prime minister from 1957 to 1960, subsequently becoming the first elected republican executive president of the West African nation from 1960 to 1966, the year his government was overthrown in a coup d'etat on February 24. In his heyday, Nkrumah was seen as a foremost Pan-Africanist. In fact, he is always remembered as having echoed the memorable words quoted above on the night that Ghana attained independence from Great Britain (on March 6, 1957) and, in the process, changed the country's name from the Gold Coast to Ghana. He displayed his Pan-Africanist spirit when he loudly proclaimed that the independence of Ghana, which he spearheaded in a volatile anti-colonialist struggle, "is meaningless unless it is linked [up] with the total liberation of the African continent."[2] Furthermore, it was in a true Pan-African spirit at a 1961 African continental conference, in the Moroccan capital of Casablanca, that President Nkrumah, *inter alia*, said unambiguously to the thunderous applause of his listeners:

> If we do not formulate plans for unity and take active steps to form [a] political union, we will soon be fighting and warring among ourselves, with imperialists and colonialists standing behind the screen and pulling vicious wires, to make us cut each other's throats for the sake of their diabolical purposes in Africa. . . . I can see no security for African states unless African leaders like ourselves have realized beyond all doubt[s] that salvation for Africa lies in unity.[3]

The foregoing statement, made by Nkrumah, showed him as a pioneering champion of African unity and as a foremost Pan-Africanist. Sierra Leone–born professor Abdul Karim Bangura in his very important 508-page tome titled *Falolaism: The Epistemologies and Methodologies of Africana Knowledge* (CAP 2019) found it necessary to dig into the true meaning of Pan-Africanism. There, he succinctly wrote that "the term Pan-Africanism implies, etymologically speaking, [that] the continent of Africa taken as a whole, can be understood in both a broader and a narrower sense."[4]

Although the Ghanaian president (Nkrumah) publicly espoused Pan-Africanism, he was not its founder. Instead, Pan-Africanism was in its formative years in the early 1900s when Nkrumah was basically a little village boy back in the Gold Coast. However, Pan-Africanism, as a burgeoning movement, did not have the stature that it currently possesses in the context of Africana studies, politics, and history. In an evolutionary manner, the movement has acquired its significance among Black political leaders, activists, and Africana scholars, due to the hard work of George Padmore (1903–1959), its foremost pioneering influence, who was born on June 28, 1903 at Arouca, Trinidad (a part of Trinidad and Tobago).

Padmore, who was named at birth as Malcolm Ivan Meredith Nurse, has been dubbed the father of modern Pan-Africanism. In this chapter, the plan is to discuss Pan-Africanism in varied forms, beginning with this abstract as introductory remark and followed by a definition to elucidate the movement. Applying historical-*cum*-sociological research tools, the entry in the *Oxford Encyclopedia* also probes Pan-Africanism in the contexts of political history; meaning as well as strands, phases, evolution, and emphases. In addition to an overview of Pan-Africanism within the neoliberal perspective, we have also endeavored to situate the movement in a variety of modern contexts, including the nuanced meaning embedded in the charter of the Organization of African Unity (OAU), now the African Union (AU).

Apart from Caribbean-born Padmore (*née* Nurse), who is significantly credited for the founding and promotion of Pan-Africanism, other Black leaders credited with the sharpening of modern-era Pan-Africanism—in their own diverse activist ways in postcolonial Africa and also among diasporan Black leaders—are such personalities as William Edward Burghardt DuBois (popularly known as W.E.B. DuBois; 1868–1963); Edward Wilmot Blyden (1832–1912); Cyril Lionel Robert James (popularly known as C.L.R. James, 1901–1989); and Kwame Ture (*née* Stokely Carmichael, 1941–1998). A vigorous new meaning in the interpretation of Pan-Africanism is the work of Dr. Bangura in his important study of Professor Toyin Falola's philosophical ideas and intellectual dispositions (i.e., *Falolaism* CAP 2019). In his crucial study, he adds a dimension that argues that the activist and intellectual roles of the foregoing Black leaders and several others should count if Pan-Africanism is to be seen as African-centeredness, adding, among other details, the following cogent explanation in this seminal publication.

From the preceding definitions, it is evident that African-centeredness presupposes knowledge of a commonality of cultural traits among the diverse peoples of Africa, which characterize and constitute a worldly view that is somehow distinct from that of the foreign worldviews that have influenced African peoples. African-centeredness simply means that the universe is a collection of relationships, and an individual or a group being in that universe is defined by and dependent upon these relationships.[5]

In Pan-Africanist terms, with African-centeredness as a context, Professor Bangura further theorized that many Black leaders have contributed to the conception and realization of African-centeredness, yet he also focused on Dr. DuBois and Nkrumah. In addition, he stressed the names of other Black leaders such as Senegalese-born Cheikh Anta Diop (1923–1986) and Guyanese-born Ivan Van Sertima (1935–2009).[6] In the realm of African-centeredness, this chapter situates the two-term electoral victories (i.e., the initial election and his re-election four years later) of former Illinois Senator Barack Hussein Obama as the first African American president of the United States within the parameters of Pan-Africanism. This is done with certain topical nuances in mind, including shortcomings in postcolonial Africa at which the so-called true Pan-Africanists have frowned at, coupled with what we deemed to be hypocrisy; for example, there are situations where Pan-African adherents are also found to be wanting in certain fronts. These have often included situations in which there is lack of equity in salaries and job opportunities for women in African countries headed by diehard Pan-Africanists. However, as reported from varied quarters, things seemed to have changed for the better for women in Malawi and Liberia, when fellow women became presidents: Joyce Banda (born on April 12, 1950) ruled Malawi as an appointed president, and served from May 2009 to April 2012, while Ellen Johnson Sirleaf (born on October 29, 1938) ruled Liberia from 2006 to 2018 as the elected president.

In the context of Pan-Africanism being perceived in African-centeredness terms, several young African leaders, including those who seized power through coups d'etat, are deemed to be true Pan-Africanists. An example was Burkina Faso's young radical and much-loved President Thomas Sankara. At the time that Sankara was reportedly assassinated by his second-in-command (Captain Blaise Compaoré), it was noted by Ernest Harsch in the highly praised publication *African Leaders of the Twentieth Century*, by Ohio University Press in 2015, that the Burkinabe leader's "[Pan-African] ideas were clearly starting to reach a new generation."[7]

Interestingly, at the time Sankara was assassinated on Thursday, October 15, 1987—barely four years after his 1983 coup—the state-owned daily newspaper *Sidwaya*, which was in support of his assassin (Compaoré), felt compelled to acknowledge that Sankara was viewed as a Pan-African hero within Burkina Faso and across the continent [of Africa]. The paper placed him in the same league with figures such as Marcus Garvey, Kwame Nkrumah, Malcolm X, Patrice Lumumba, Sékou Touré, and Cheick Anta Diop. "Twenty years after his death," the newspaper commented, "his Pan-Africanist ideas remain intact in the memory of Africa's peoples, in particular its youth."[8] A very useful discussion of Nkrumah's Pan-Africanist zeal has, most recently, been offered by Smith College Africana Professor Jeffrey S. Ahlman in his book *Living With Nkrumahism: Nation State and Pan-Africanism in Ghana*, published in 2017 by Ohio University Press.[9]

PAN-AFRICANISM: DIVERSE DEFINITIONS AND INTERPRETATIONS

Pan-Africanism has been defined and depicted in diverse ways by different scholars due to its broad scope as an idea and movement, as it thrived and flourished in different historical periods, regions, and continents of the world. In *Encyclopedia of Race and Racism* (2nd edition), this movement (which evolved as an idea) has been characterized in the following words: "Pan-Africanism sought to unite Africans and overcome ethnicity by stressing the similarities and connections among all Africans. Pan-Africanism emphasizes black pride and African identity and sought to unite Africans with their kin in the diaspora."[10]

What can be deduced from this definition is that, by virtue of their race, Black people have been oppressed through enslavement, colonization as well as imperialism and their attendant modern form known as neocolonialism. In the process, they have been treated as purchasable properties instead of being seen as fellow human beings. Instead, they are considered inferior to other races who become their oppressors. Indeed, this obvious shared experience of oppression and marginalization culminated in the rallying cry for change by the Pan-African movement espoused by radical African political leaders and Black conscious nationalists, led by Trinidad's Padmore. They sought this change in the context of decolonization on the African continent and in the Black diaspora, including the Caribbean. In the context of the foregoing definition, there are two broad categories which characterize the word that is redefined as a social movement.[11] Black scholars in the diaspora and those based on the African continent, indeed, are seen as two broad groups that would eventually influence each other at different degrees and levels of intensity depending on the specific historical era, coupled by the vision and scope of engagement of particular social actors in the overall movement. Thus, by interpretation, for Africans in the diaspora, the key focus of Pan-Africanist activities is to fight against racism, injustice, and systematic social exclusion based on race and national origin.

On the other hand, for Africans living on the continent, whose leaders in the late 1940s and 1950s spearheaded the decolonization struggles, Pan-Africanism was seen as a platform for Africans to unite against European colonial rule, coupled with the domination and oppression of Africans on grounds of their racial and national origin or ethnicity. In the foregoing contexts, varied definitions have been ascribed to or propounded for the Pan-African movement as it is known today. For example, a definition of Pan-Africanism can be found in *The Columbia Electronic Encyclopedia (6th Edition)*, which provides its readers with the following interpretation of the movement:

> Pan-Africanism is a general term for various movements in Africa that have as their common goal the unity of Africans and the elimination of colonialism and white supremacy from the continent. However, on the scope and meaning of Pan-Africanism, including such matters as leadership, political orientation, and national as opposed to regional interests, they are widely, often bitterly, divide.[12]

Furthermore, the Columbia encyclopedic volume's definition goes a long way to raise specters of some wide-ranging conceptual problems as well as issues which are worthy of notification as the movement (or Pan-Africanism) is redefined in the 21st century. Therefore, in many respects, Pan-Africanism is seen as a movement that is either reeking or reacting against injustice not only at Africans on the continent, but also the tumultuous Black populace based in the wide diasporic spectrum. In the foregoing context, activists are often seen to be much more united in what they oppose than their final destination in terms of the vision of the ideal future. This is, indeed, not surprising; for, according to Thomas Hobbes, it is not unusual that people may agree on the existence of God and do believe in just that. Yet, they may equally disagree on what is the best way to worship Him (God).[13] It is similar to how some people may just believe in Pan-Africanism as a broad idea but, in the final process, disagree fundamentally in the details. A second example may suffice in the fact that although Black people have historically been oppressed on the home front in Africa and in different parts of the world, including the United States, they have also been subjugated and denied full human dignity in general and human rights in particular.

Just as Padmore (Caribbean), Malcolm X (the United States, 1925–1965), Kwame Nkrumah (Ghana, 1909–1972), Sekou Toure (Guinea, 1922–1984), and other Pan-Africanists have concluded, it must be conceded that the non-Black oppressors, for many years, used a divide-and-conquer tactic, with the level of oppression not experienced in the same degree by all of the Black groups.[14] This is why Pan-Africanism, as an idea, has incarnated in different kinds of movements and organizations, with many of their activities representing the concrete challenges and struggles of particular regions or periods of history. It is for this reason that there are disagreements among some of the leaders of the movement. Even when they agree on the goals of the movement, they may disagree on the best strategy to achieve or realize such eventualities (or goals).

For an overall understanding of the theory and practice of Pan-Africanism, there are two other conceptual issues that we endeavor to address. Just as it is done in the instance of historicity, there is the need for periodization of the tenets of the movement in order to decide when it started, and what kind of political action or organization qualifies to be called Pan-Africanist.[15] At this juncture, we can underscore that there are many political actions aimed at fighting both perceived and real injustice, but the final analysis is to decide whether or not they do qualify to be categorized under the canopy of Pan-Africanism. With regard to timing or periodization, the key issue is whether or not an individual considers the existence of Pan-Africanism from when it was either a sentiment or a concretization of a political organization defining and redefining itself as Pan-Africanist. In this respect, it is fair to conclude that, since no concrete organization comes into existence without an idea preceding it, the origin of Pan-Africanism can best be traced back to the time when Black people globally developed a unified sentiment or consciousness against their oppression, discrimination, and domination by non-Black entities. This was subsequently followed by concrete organizing in the form of anti-colonialist as well as anti-imperialist and anti-racist struggles, spearheaded by nationalists in Africa and radical activists in Europe and the United States.

Political Prism and Meaning of Pan-Africanism

With regard to the types of political actions by Black men and women in and outside Africa, which would constitute Pan-Africanism, Esedebe in his very useful published work *Pan-Africanism: The Idea and Movement, 1776–1991* was of the view that not every kind of political action qualifies to be included in the family of Pan-Africanism. He further offered a clarification that although in 1896, Bai Bureh, a Sierra Leonean nationalist, led a revolt against what was seen as House Tax in his West African nation, which was founded by the British to settle its freed slaves, such a revolt did not qualify as a Pan-African political action. However, Esedebe in fact hailed from the Igbo ethnic group of Nigeria, which was the birthplace of the 1929 Women's War that has been brilliantly discussed by Professor Nwando Achebe and others; yet, the Women's War in the former Southeastern area of Nigeria did not qualify as a Pan-Africanist political action as observers never saw an African-centeredness in the event.

After all, in the context of Pan-Africanism, Esedebe has further underscored that his conclusions were based on the fact that the Aba Women's Riot (dubbed as Women's War earlier), which was similar to the Bureh-led revolt in Sierra Leone, for example, was essentially concerned with the narrow interests of their communities and geographical locations, but not with the wider Pan-Africanist worldview. Consequently, Esedebe theorized that only events as well as people, whose ideas and actions are associated with the ideals of Pan-Africanism as a movement in its broader scope, deserve to be recognized as being Pan-Africanist, often with only men being seen at the vanguard of the movement. However, that would be contrary to the depiction by Dr.Nwando Achebe, endowed history professor at Michigan State University, who identified female warriors in her seminal study, *Farmers, Traders, Warriors and Kings: Female Power and Authority in Northern Igboland, 1900–1960* (Heinemann, 2005).[16]

In the foregoing respect, Nkrumah, as Ghana's post-independent leader, distinguished himself, in his lifetime, as a true Pan-Africanist because of his various continental-level actions, including the memorable maiden statement on March 6, 1957 during the celebration of Ghana's independence from British colonial rule as well as his subsequent active involvement in the creation, in 1963 in Addis Ababa, Ethiopia, of the OAU, now the AU. Aside from these noble actions, on the part of Nkrumah, he went on to write extensively in monographs about and published long essays on his understanding of Pan-Africanism. His writings promoted Ghanaian culture in the context of what he described as the African personality, indeed seeing it as an element for redefining the tenets of Pan-Africanism or, as Professor Bangura would see it, Africa-centeredness.

At this juncture, Distinguished Professor Falola comes to mind, as he is also quoted in *Falolaism* by Bangura for his very perceptive publication on aspects of imperialism in *Nationalism and African Intellectuals*. Here, he is acknowledged as having, *inter alia*, stated that African cultural nationalists did have a "radical" comprehension of imperialism, hence "they argued that superior technology made the European invasion of Africa possible."[17]

In the final analysis, the concept of Pan-Africanism differs from person to person, sometimes depending on an individual's social, political, and economic background. Nonetheless, Esedebe is subsequently of the view that although the term Pan-Africanism did not come into use until after 1900, the sentiment behind the idea could, in historical perspective, still be traced back to the U.S. Declaration of Independence in 1776. To the Nigerian Pan-Africanist writer, the consequence of that declaration led to the abolitionist movements of the time, coupled with the radical reaction of free Blacks outside Africa, especially as a prelude to the 1884–1885 Berlin Conference, which culminated in the partitioning of Africa into spheres of Eurocentric interests.

To a large extent, what the foregoing nuances confirm is that the notion of Pan-Africanism did not emanate from continental Africa but in the so-called New World, where Blacks commenced the fight for their human dignity and against the colossal evils of systematic oppression, enslavement, overall exploitation, and covert and overt discrimination. The Pan-Africanist struggle in the Black diaspora, spearheaded by Padmore, Blyden, DuBois, and others, would later spread like a wild bush fire to the African continent. For example, in the United States, Malcolm X, the radical Black leader and Muslim activist, felt so enraged by the shabby treatment of post-emancipation freed Blacks that he threatened to drag the United States before such world and regional bodies as the United Nations, the erstwhile OAU, AU, and the International Court of Justice in The Hague.[18]

PAN-AFRICANISM: STRANDS, PHASES, EVOLUTION, AND EMPHASES

As it has been emphasized, Pan-Africanism is not an easy undertaking that can be covered exhaustively, mostly because events that shape and promote it are in different places, regions, and times. Again, it is also a fact that Pan-Africanism flourished in different regions of the world, including Europe, Africa, and North America. That is why in our study we have chosen to provide a brief and general overview as well as the inspiration for the beginning of the idea as a burgeoning movement. However, in the end, we have focused on how it spread to the African continent, and how, in the final analysis, it is currently thriving and being promoted in a variety of ways in the 21st century, especially in countries where the consciousness of the citizenry was sharpened by postcolonial leaders, but not in African countries where neocolonialism—new colonialist exploitation as discussed in publications by Nkrumah and others—has subsequently assumed tap root status in the absence of active colonialism.

Although there is a broadly shared commitment and ideals among Pan-Africanists, President Paul Zeleza of the American University of Kenya has brilliantly identified six different strands of Pan-Africanism. To him, each of the six strands was either enamored or promoted by a particular kind of social imaginary. The first strand is called "Trans-Atlantic Pan-Africanism," which identified the unique commitment of a group of scholars whose overall interests included building the movement to serve as a connection and a bridge between the Black people of continental Africa and those in the diaspora world of North and South America. The second group is known as "Black-Atlantic Pan-Africanism" because the focus of their scholarship and social organizing is restricted to the African diasporic communities that exist in the United States and Britain, totally excluding Blacks on the African continent and Latin America.[19]

Meanwhile, an example of scholarship in this tradition is the monograph *The Black Atlantic* by Paul Gilroy. In this publication, Gilroy only celebrates the achievements, creative successes, and accomplishments of Blacks in the United States and Britain. In doing so, he ignored the Africa-based Black citizenry that forms the bulk of the Black race in general. The third form of Pan-Africanism is known as "Continental Pan-Africanism," which has its main concern and focus centered on how the continent of Africa can be united. This group has as its romanticized hero in Ghana's late president Kwame Nkrumah, who wrote *Africa Must Unite* to promote the Pan-Africanist ideal. He also teamed up with several of his Pan-African colleagues such as Julius Nyerere (Tanzania), Ahmed Sekou Toure (Guinea), Modibo Keita (Mali) Abdel Nasser (Egypt), and several others to found and nurture the OAU in 1963, which as stated earlier is now known as the AU. The current appellation was championed fiscally and politically by the assassinated Libyan president Muammar Ghaddafi (1940–2011). He was assassinated during North Africa's Arab Spring. The fourth type of Pan-Africanism focuses only on Sub-Saharan Africa, which emerged after the deaths of Keita, Nkrumah, Toure, and other radical West African political leaders.

The fifth strand is focused on North Africa proper, but often extends itself to include the Middle East and Western Asia where migrated Blacks can be found. This ideal is sometimes characterized as Pan-Arabism. The sixth and last version of Pan-Africanism is global in scope, and it is based on the belief that it is desirable to bring together all people with shared African ancestry all over the world, similar to the Negritude movement that former Senegalese president Senghor promoted to embrace Black consciousness in Africa and in the diaspora.

Contextually, there seems to be complications which have preceded the foregoing classifications, including the fact that there are other forms of solidary communities that cut across the six strands of Pan-Africanism, sometimes creating divisions of their own and divided loyalties, which have been discussed in detail by Dr. Zaleza.[20] Also, for instance, within the African continent, there are divisions along the lines of English-speaking regions (Anglophone), French-speaking countries (Francophone), and Portuguese-speaking regions (Lusophone). Such divisions go a long way to suggest the extent of colonial legacies that can sometimes undermine a shared African heritage. Furthermore, it has been a long-standing and unfortunate fact that in early post-independent Africa, some brands of Pan-Africanism were elite-driven, while others were populist in orientation.

There have also been Pan-Africanists, who are reformist in thinking, while others are simply radical like Burkina Faso's assassinated President Thomas Sankara (1949–1987), Ghana's former president J.J. Rawlings (1947–), and others. Above all, there was for instance individuals who merely emphasized the shared experience of being Black and oppressed, including African American leaders like Malcolm X, who is discussed in detail in *Malcolm X: A Biography* (2014) and *Malcolm X and Africa* (2016) both of which were co-authored by A.B. Assensoh and Yvette M. Alex-Assensoh. These individuals are accommodating of capitalism, while others are inspired by Marxist vision of class analysis, inequality, and history. Both ideological strata have often divided people with similar aspirations, even if they are of the same racial stock. Such Pan-Africanists are committed to the creation of a socialist society within the Pan-African milieu. Then, some Pan-Africanist social movements circumscribe their organizing interests within their nation while others are transnational. Finally, there are some individuals and their organizations whose organizing is framed within the context of their ethnic groups, which makes them parochial and limited in the overall scope of Pan-Africanism.

PAN-AFRICANISM IN BLACK POLITICAL HISTORY

Historically, it is important to conclude unequivocally that the first wave of Pan-Africanist thought started in the Black diaspora in the 18th century, led by such notable figures as Prince Hall (of the Prince Hall's Black Masonic fame), Edward Wilmot Blyden, Paul Cuffe (or Cuffey), Martin Delany, Henry McNeal Turner, and Alfred Charles (Chief) Sam. One of the essential goals of these pioneering Pan-Africanists was to bring back the descendants of slaves to Africa under what later became the clarion cry of the 1920s by Jamaican-born Marcus Garvey through the "Back to Africa" movement. They had wide-ranging motivations, which included political, financial, and religious aspirations.[21]

For many of the pioneers of the movement, whether explicitly or implicitly stated, bringing Christianity and the so-called civilization to Africa was the key focal concern of their brand of Pan-Africanism. The perception of this cohort of Pan-Africanists, with its focus on returning to Africa as freed men and women, can be deduced from the kind of nomenclature they used to depict Africa. Based on their language, their views can clearly be said to resemble colonial ideas about Africa that were previously dominant among Europeans at the time. For instance, here is what Martin Delaney had to say about Liberia as part of his conception of Africa:

The regeneration of the African race can only be effected by its own efforts, the efforts of its own self, whatever aid may come from other sources; and it must in this venture succeed, as God leads the movement and his hands guides the way. And now the advanced civilization of the Christianity of the world is called upon to recognize and overture to their consideration.[22]

Given Delaney's type of reasoning, it is not surprising that the harsh treatment meted out to native ethnic groups of Liberia by returning freed slaves, who called themselves Americo-Liberians, was based on an ideology similar to that which informed the treatment of native Black people of Africa by their colonizers. As time went on, the Christianizing emphasis diminished as the emancipated Blacks zealously pursued Pan-Africanist ideas, including plans to return to Africa, in varied ways with strategies to redeem the continent. The sentiment, indeed, remained in the social imagination of the Black political elites, especially those with radical predispositions. A turning point in the movement was the Pan-African Congress of 1900 which took place in London. During this Congress, Black leaders from many parts of the colonized world and across other national boundaries in Europe and the Americas gathered and collaborated under the leadership of Henry Sylvester Williams from Trinidad and Tobago, who was a lawyer by training. The objectives and aims of the 1900 Pan-African Congress were enunciated in the following points:

Secure to Africans throughout the world true civil and political rights.

To ameliorate the condition of our brothers on the continent of Africa, America and other parts of the world.

To promote the efforts to secure effective legislation and encourage our people in educational, industrial and commercial enterprises.

To foster the production of writing and statistics relating to our people everywhere. To raise funds for forwarding these purposes.[23]

Indeed, what was notable about this Congress was the lack of representation of people from continental Africa, mainly because in 1900, almost all of the countries were still under colonial yoke. Although the organizing leadership (led by Henry Sylvester Williams) was no longer at the organization's helm at the time another Pan-African Congress was held in Manchester in 1945, his work inspired others to pursue the initiative for subsequent Pan-African Congresses; the successor was Dr. DuBois of the United States, who in the 1960s migrated to Ghana to add Ghanaian citizenship to that of his American citizenship (an idea of a dual citizenship). The context for DuBois's engagement with Pan-Africanism and the future evolution of the movement in the early part of the 20th century was eventually shaped by the impact of the First World War of 1914 on the movement. One of the impacts of the War on Pan-Africanism was that it created a context for increased contact among Africans on the continent and those in the diaspora.[24] They found themselves in a cosmopolitan environment all of them from diverse social backgrounds. African Americans met Blacks from the French Empire to dialogue with each other. This was because France forcefully recruited soldiers from French colonies in Africa including Senegal and Sudan and from the French Caribbean to fight on her side during that war. Consequently, France became the center of collaboration among Blacks from different parts of the world between the two World Wars.

In fact, African residents and Black students in France formed literary and philosophical groups and associations. Similar associations were formed in the United Kingdom and collaborated with those in France. Several members of the movement left France for the United Kingdom considering Britain as a more suitable base. Active members of the Harlem Renaissance engaged in close contact with Black people from the French colonial empire.[25] It was during this inter-war period in France that the Negritude movement, espoused by Leopold Sedar Senghor, had its formative impact. Negritude simply translated means "Blackness" or "Black essence." The goal of the movement was to elevate the identity of Black people as a group. Blacks were never to be ashamed of themselves or feel inferior to any racial group, but be proud of who they were.[26] Negritude also provided a systematic critique of European colonialism. To properly appreciate the impact of the movement, one has to identify its two broad factions including the stance of each strand: the moderate versus the radical factions.

Negritude, which would subsequently play a useful role in promoting some aspects of Pan-Africanism, was divided into factions. For example, the moderate faction of Negritude was led by the then-president Leopold Sedar Senghor of Senegal (1906–2001), who was the West African country's first elected democratic leader, serving from 1960 to 1980. Although he believed in Negritude, while in office, Senghor promoted close political, economic, and cultural ties with France after independence.[27] On the other hand, the radical faction of this movement similar to Pan-Africanism, was led by Aime Cesaire from the French colony of Martinique. Cesaire, who was a deputy in the National Assembly of France, published a monograph titled *Discourse on Colonialism* (in 1955), in which he absolutely condemned European civilization as embarrassingly hypocritical because, in his opinion, they claimed to fight war for democracy, while they imposed colonial domination on other people in Africa and the Caribbean. In brief, he characterized European civilization as morally and ethically duplicitous in the ideals they claimed, as their performance ran counter to these ideals.[28]

Invariably, there were certain insights from the Negritude movement that were indicators of both the progressive potential of Pan-Africanism and practical challenges in its epistemic conceptualization and understanding of Blackness, coupled with the strategy that it inspired the movement's leaders throughout the continent of Africa and some parts of Europe, notably France and the United Kingdom. Conceptually, the Negritude movement from its beginning was built on the expectations of the ideals of Nkrumah's African personality, culture, and history. The presumption was that this understanding would form the basis on which all Africans could feel dignified and proud of their singular racial identity and ancestry, culminating in a social movement on the basis of such insights.[29]

The preceding line of reasoning was at one point or another manifested in the thinking of some postcolonial African leaders' who in some respect identified the pre-colonial African cultural heritage as either communal or family-oriented (Ujamaa, as reflected in Tanzania by the then-president Julius K. Nyerere).[30] A constructive critique of this line of reasoning that is embedded in the Negritude movement was put forward by Paulin J. Hountondji (1942-). For him, it was a false premise to begin a conceptual framework for building Africa's future by naively accepting as fact that there was one African cultural identity or one singular African personality that is, the "unanimist" presumption. Also, for him, Africa has always been and would continue to be a culturally pluralistic continent.[31] It never had a system of values that was totally homogeneous. In brief, Africa was to be seen as diverse and pluralistic. Along this line of reasoning, the late distinguished public intellectual and professor of political science and cultural anthropology Ali A. Mazrui (1933–2014) described Africa as a product of a triple heritage, often using himself as an example, due to his varied identities as an African (with an Arabic descent), a Muslim, and a Western-educated individual.[32] It is in fact, not surprising that Professor Mazrui, with his triple heritage, did excel so much as an intellectual and author that, since his death in 2014, he has been dubbed "Black [George] Orwell," as espoused in the 2018 edited volume *Black Orwell: Essays on the Scholarship of Ali A. Mazrui*, co-edited by Drs. Seifuden Adem formerly of Binghamton, New York and Kimani Njogu of Nairobi, Kenya, both of whom knew Dr. Mazrui and his widow, Nigerian-born Mrs. Pauline Mazrui, very well.[33]

Pan-Africanism in the Inter-War Years, 1914 and 1945

Continuing with the dynamics of how the inter-war years (1914 and 1945, respectively) shaped Pan-Africanism as a growing ideological ideal of Black intellectuals and the elite, it must be noted that self-determination became an important issue of concern among the colonized people during this period.[34]

Although Dr. DuBois, for example, was an American, his scholarly work and political activism changed due to the influences of the cosmopolitan Black diaspora community that was in France. Thus, with blessings from Blaise Diagne (1872–1934), who was at the time a Deputy of the French National Assembly representing Senegal and later becoming Mayor of Dakar; with his help, his friend (Dr. DuBois) organized a Pan-African Congress in 1919 in Paris.[35]

Dr. DuBois, who saw European colonial mission and domination as the core explanation for why World War I was fought, was indeed more militant in his approach to the ideals of Pan-Africanism than earlier leaders of the movement up to this time. DuBois adopted a more radical tone as it could be deduced from the resolution produced at the end of the 1919 Pan-African Congress in Paris, which he organized. The following is a part of the resolution: "The natives of Africa must have the right to participate in government as fast as their development permit."[36]

Subsequent Pan-African Congresses were held in London, Paris, and Brussels in 1921. One of the high demands of the second Pan-African Congress of 1921 was: "The return of Negroes to their land and its natural fruits, and defense against unrestrained greed of invested capital." There were eight demands altogether that were made by the Congress.[37] It was at this moment, in the 1920s, that Dr. DuBois's sentiment shifted away from the National Association for the Advancement of Colored Peoples (NAACP) in the United States to Black Internationalism in the context of Pan-Africanism. It was also in the 1920s that DuBois encountered a great rival to his mission of Pan-Africanism in the Jamaican Marcus Garvey and his United Negro Improvement Association (UNIA). The UNIA had branches in more than 40 African countries, represented in the commercial print media, that is, in Nigeria, Liberia, Sierra Leone, and Mozambique. The UNIA, unlike early Pan-Africanist movements with the Black consciousness approach, was not interested in Christianizing Africa. The movement wanted to unify all African colonies and people into one nation. The presumption was that Marcus Garvey would, at the time, eventually become the president of the United States of Africa.[38]

Meanwhile, one of the unique contributions of UNIA members was that their activities and ideas were now accessible to Africans on the continent, especially young Africans, who later led the nationalist movement on the continent. However, through the efforts of J. Edgar Hoover, the FBI director in the United States, Garvey would be arrested, tried, and convicted of mail fraud, imprisoned and eventually deported. In spite of this setback, Garvey's vision, as incarnated in the UNIA, would inspire people in the West Indies, African Americans living under the tyranny of Jim Crow, and Africans living under colonial domination.[39] His diction, with regard to Africa had such phrases like "Africa for Africans," inspired people to think of forming organizations that cut across nations based on the shared solidarity of oppressed Black people.

BLACK LEADERSHIP AND RELEVANCE TO PAN-AFRICANISM

It is in the foregoing context that the late president Nkrumah of Ghana and his generation became relevant to the next level of Pan-Africanism as a movement. In Nkrumah's home base, in the former Gold Coast (Ghana since March 6, 1957), and in many other African countries, during the inter-war period, there was great agitation for self-determination, which was accompanied by the deteriorating returns from cash crops, such as cocoa in Ghana[40] Many of the African veterans of the First World War who fought on behalf of the Allied Forces returned to the continent with new perspectives about the world, race relations, and the potential achievements of their kith and kin. They recalled that when they, as African soldiers participated in the war side by side with their European counterparts, they still experienced bias. However, the war disabused their minds, as African soldiers, of the myth of inherent White superiority and invincibility, as some of the African soldiers fought more gallantly than their European and White American counterparts. This is because they realized that the White man was an ordinary human being who could equally be killed by a single bullet.

So, while the Allied nations won the war, the war generated demand for increasing democratization in the African continent which was predominantly under colonial rule. For instance, in 1920, there was a conference in West Africa at which professionals and wage laborers made demands on the colonial government in Ghana. By 1935, there were many African students with nationalist inspiration studying in Western universities, including Nkrumah and the late Dr. Nnamdi Azikiwe of Nigeria who were educated at Lincoln University in Pennsylvania and later became the first presidents of their countries (Ghana and Nigeria, respectively). Lincoln University, their Pennsylvania-based college with Pan-Africanist leaders and interests is a historically Black university.[41] Nkrumah, who was considered the father of continental African Pan-Africanism, attended the institution from 1935 to 1940 earning a BA degree in sociology and a sacred theology degree from its Theology College. He later pursued Graduate Studies at the University of Pennsylvania from where he earned two master's degree in Education and Philosophy, but was unable to complete the dissertation for his doctoral (PhD) degree at the institution before he left the United States for good to live in the United Kingdom.

During his time in the United States, Nkrumah like many other African students, came face to face with racial discrimination and segregation in the form of Jim Crowism. Nkrumah also spent some time in Harlem in New York City, where he countered numerous people espousing diverse Pan-Africanist ideas.[42] As Nkrumah lived abroad, his ideas and perspectives about life were shaped and molded by varied experiences. His nationalist aspirations, at this time, were redefined, and his former professor from Lincoln stated, *inter alia*: "No matter what a paper was supposed to be on, Nkrumah always twisted it around to write on African freedom and anti-colonial struggle."[43] Thus, Nkrumah would make sure that he converted every writing assignment to something he could write about Africa. The kind of education Nkrumah received abroad impacted him significantly like many other students from various African countries. Nkrumah was on record confessing to having been influenced by his studies in the United States with regard to his Pan-African vision and understanding of the world and Africa's place in it. His observation was the following: "During my stay in America the conviction was firmly created in me that a great deal in their thought could assist us in the fight against colonialism."[44] Some of the works that were referenced here were the revolutionary writings of Karl Marx, George Friederich Hegel, and Vladimir Lenin, which were strongly recommended to him by C.L.R. James, a radical West Indian or Caribbean. Nkrumah also asserted that "But I think that of all the literature that I studied, the book that did more than any other to fire my enthusiasm was *The Philosophy and Opinions of Marcus Garvey*."[45]

Just as there was Pan-African political organizing in the United States, a similar one was afoot in Europe. Nkrumah—upon completing his studies in the United States—proceeded to London for further studies. There, he met George Padmore, a former avowed Communist, who was from Trinidad and Tobago.[46] Like other future African leaders, Nkrumah encountered the political ideas and movements that espoused Pan-African and anti-colonial thought which started after the First World War. At the time Nkrumah arrived in the United Kingdom, discussion in Pan-African circles on Negritude was quickly transformed into dialogue about nationalism and anti-colonial movements. This was escalated by the Second World War with public rhetoric and discourses condemning fascism. There was also the release of the Atlantic Charter in 1941, which allowed colonized people to pursue self-determination at the end of the war.[47]

The next Pan-African Congress that would constitute a watershed in the movement from the perspective of Africans on the continent and Blacks in the diaspora was held in 1945 in Manchester in the United Kingdom. This Congress became a turning point for African students studying in Europe in general and the United Kingdom in particular. The key theme that emerged was the liberation of Africa building on earlier steps to Pan-African nationalism in the United States. In attendance at the Manchester Congress were such Black leaders as: Wallace Johnson (Sierra Leone), Jomo Kenyatta

(Kenya), and Nnamdi Azikiwe, Obafemi Awolowo, and Jaja Nwachuku (all from Nigeria). Nkrumah and Kenyatta were joint-secretaries for the Congress.[48]

It is important to note that while the Pan-African Congress held in 1900 was attended by only two Africans, who were entrepreneurs, the 1945 Congress had many African students; Nkrumah's role at the 1945 Pan-African Congress was spectacular, as he made appropriate contributions to the event radicalizing many African students and workers which saw them commit to the anti-colonial struggle for the freedom of the whole of Africa. Nkrumah is known to have written two declarations that were adopted by the 1945 Congress. The main Congress declaration was: "The Declaration to the Colonial Peoples of the World," and the second one was "Declaration to Colonial Workers, Farmers and Intellectuals."[49] These declarations introduced new demands and dimensions to the anti-colonial struggle and the Pan-Africanist movement. The declarations also introduced a new level of consciousness and radical sentiment among the people in West Africa engaged in nationalist struggles. Nkrumah's role at the conference demonstrated how his exposure to Western social and political education decisively transformed his worldview as well as his way of thinking for the betterment of Africa. It must also be noted that it did not make him Eurocentric but, instead, stimulated his mind and thinking for the need for contextualization of knowledge, whatever its source. Moreover, his role in the conference supported by the man who later became Kenya's first leader—President Jomo Kenyatta—demonstrated beyond reasonable doubt that he had the capacity to mobilize people from different social and cultural backgrounds to identify with and participate in the Pan-Africanist struggle.

In addition to actively participating by helping to organize and to shape the Manchester Pan-African Congress of 1945, Nkrumah also became active in creating an organization named "The Circle," which included numerous African students committed to the promotion of national unity and an independent union of African Socialist Republic.[50] While in England, Nkrumah's deep interest in Pan-Africanism saw him aligning with other political organizations such as the West African National Secretariat with the aim of influencing the Labor Party and the Fabian Colonial Bureau to make pro-Africa policies.[51] Nkrumah, Kenyatta, and other students from colonial countries of Africa in Europe, at that time, would later return to Africa to provide vanguard leadership that would result in the independence of the great majority of African countries from colonial rule by the end of the 1960s.[52] Nkrumah used his experience to organize a Pan-African conference in 1958 in the Ghanaian capital of Accra, which was attended by other future African leaders from various postcolonial African countries. Several factions emerged with regard to the best way to achieve Pan-African unity. The key difference was how fast Pan-African ideals were to be pursued and the scope of the cooperation among African countries.[53]

In many respects, postcolonial African leaders became too committed to defending the national boundaries of their nations bequeathed to them by the European colonial rulers. Many, therefore, did not want to forfeit their privileges as presidents or prime ministers in their newly independent countries in pursuance of universal continental unity the ultimate goal of Pan-Africanism. Often, with few exceptions, the postcolonial nations embraced the capitalist method of development, which meant that they were competing among themselves, resulting in what analysts would consider a zero-sum game. Those that embraced African socialism ignored the fact that there were no shortcuts to progress. In fact, Rene Dumont, the French scholar, was encouraged to write a critique titled *False Start in Africa*.[54] Also, Paulin Hountondji argued against the premise that all pre-colonial Africans shared a singular African culture, stating that those who held this view were not just naïve but factually wrong.[55]

Pan-Africanism and its adherents steered clear of ideological influences, especially after its father George Padmore abandoned his Communist affiliation. However, many social contradictions emerged under African socialism.[56] The primary focus of most postcolonial African leaders became national development, conceived within the framework of individual postcolonial nations. The then-president Nkrumah, who devoted much of his time to Pan-Africanist ideals, was not appreciated very much by some strong-willed Ghanaian elites, who conspired with military and police officers to overthrow his government in 1966. He thereby paid a huge political price in 1966 for his Pan-Africanist commitment.

PAN-AFRICANISM AND THE POSTCOLONIAL STATE

In view of the ideals that Pan-Africanists like Nkrumah and others want to achieve in the context of postcolonial Africa, it is legitimate to wonder today how that can be accomplished, especially given the presence of the postcolonial state and the nature of the elites, who run the institution necessary for the realization of the same ideals. Some of these have become neocolonial stooges and agents. To arrive at a thorough understanding of this, it is important to examine the nature and inner-workings of the postcolonial state in Africa. Toward that end, several scholars continue to argue that the postcolonial state was overdeveloped because it was imposed from above and outside and not as a product of the normal evolution of African culture and people.[57] As historical-*cum*-political facts have amply demonstrated, colonial rulers and their masters governed Africa in a harsh as well as an unequal and unfair manner. Not only was the goal of colonial rulers to exploit Africa in the interest of the colonizing nations but they governed the people and regions unevenly with divide-and-conquer intentions.[58] While the subsequent nationalist struggle for independence mobilized the masses, very often the social movements struggling for independence were heavily influenced by regional and ethnic sentiments. Consequently, even those movements that were inclusive could not ignore the ethnic and regional quagmire.[59]

In many respects, the various struggles for economic development and nation building did fall below expectations, especially given the high aspirations and expectations of the generation of that era and after. As a result, many African countries faced the problem of social dualism in their development mainly because of the simultaneous existence of developed urban centers with neglected, exploited, and backward rural communities and regions.[60] Many urban-based interest groups in the postcolonial period were more interested in pursuing narrow regional, religious, generational, class, ethnic, and petit-bourgeois commercial interests instead of national interests, let alone a Pan-African agenda envisioned by previous Pan-Africanist Congresses. Indeed, many postcolonial leaders felt insecure in their governing positions in the late 1960s and, as a result, pursued the strategy of centralization of state power, sometimes accompanied by draconian national laws. A typical example was Ghana's Preventive Detention Act (PDA), which empowered the nation to arrest and detain for as long as five years opponents of the regime, without trial or conviction. Such illegal acts, which no Pan-Africanist leader or adherent ever assumed could happen in postcolonial Africa, led to the sudden military and police overthrow of postcolonial leaders in various African nations.

In concrete terms, the centralization of state power and bureaucracy were utilized at the whim of the rulers, a travesty of preached Pan-Africanist vision. This included incapacitating competing political parties, which were often associated with regions or ethnic groups and co-opting or intimidating, detaining, or even eliminating political opponents through killer squads and militias. In some cases, elections were systematically biased and rigged. The ruling elites who felt insecure also imposed constitutional restrictions on representative democratic institutions. At the end, most postcolonial African states became patrimonial, preferring personal rule instead of an effective legal-rational mode of governance.[61]

Again, most postcolonial African governments, including Nkrumah's Ghana, became single-party systems if they were not taken over by military leaders through coups d'etat. Furthermore, the postcolonial states became characterized by increased ethnic polarization while a patron-client mode of governance became dominant.[62] While there are various explanations to account for this postcolonial situation, it clearly represents an abysmal failure from the high ideals of the well-known Pan-African Congresses. Most certainly, such levels of failure do not make Africans feel proud of themselves, let alone bold enough to compare themselves with East Asian and Western countries. Amid this feeling of insecurity among leaders and elected dictators, there was little initiative for the high ideals of Pan-Africanism to thrive and flourish, except during the struggle against White minority rule in South Africa (apartheid) and in Zimbabwe, Mozambique, and Namibia. However, as Professor Ali A. Mazrui argued, foreign rule in the southern African region was a great achievement for Africa, but also a great loss in terms of the disappearance of a common source of unity for all African countries and their citizenry. At the end, most postcolonial nations in Africa became predatory rather than developmental.[63] The problem with predatory states is that they do not create conditions for the people and the economy and other social institutions to thrive and flourish. Indeed, as prebendal states, they diminished the conditions and social climate for people's productivity and creativity.[64] The conglomeration of economic and political crises in Africa forced the countries to embrace a new brand of capitalism via structural Adjustment Program (SAP), known as neoliberal globalization. This is the subject of the next section.

PAN-AFRICANISM IN THE ERA OF NEOLIBERAL GLOBALIZATION

In the preceding section of our publication, we did argue that the Pan-Africanist project, as it was known to exist before decolonization emerged, suffered under insecure ruling elites in postcolonial Africa. Leaders were both politically desperate as well as immature, with much concern about their personal and political security than upholding and promoting the national interests, let alone Pan-Africanist ideals, as promoted by earlier selfless Black leaders. In the era of neoliberal globalization, the nature of the postcolonial state will ultimately be forced to change. This is because for the most part it would be subordinated to what critics saw as the fiscal agenda of the World Bank and the International Monetary Fund (IMF) under the hegemonic regime of the Washington Consensus brand of global capitalism.[65]

In fact, the collapse of the Berlin Wall in 1989—thanks to conservative President Ronald Reagan who advocated its collapse—represented the effective end of Communism and, to an extent, active socialism as viable social and economic systems that could be considered alternatives to capitalism. It would be recalled that many leading Pan-African leaders, with Pan-Africanist agenda and avowed interests like Nkrumah and Nyerere, did receive unlimited ideological sympathies from the Soviet Union, its satellite allies, and the People's Republic of China headed for a long time by Chairman Mao Zedong. However, by 1989, a new form of capitalism under the so-called Washington Consensus emerged. Indeed, by the mid-1980s, the great majority of African regimes were forced by deteriorating economic and political situations to embrace the SAPs of the IMF and World Bank. As the available records have shown, by 1989, only five Sub-Saharan African countries had lived within their means without borrowing money from the IMF, which had imposed stringent conditions (including SAPs) for their loans. The IMF insisted that African governments implement public policies and institutional reforms that qualitatively changed the relationship between the postcolonial leaders and ordinary citizens. Neoliberalism, which is better known in Britain as *Thatcherism* (a term coined by Jamaican-born Stuart Hall (1932–2014), a Rhodes Scholar) is, indeed, not just an economic policy and strategy but also a moral philosophy.[66]

Indeed, former conservative British prime minister Margret Thatcher (1925–2013) was quoted as having said: "Economics are the method, but the object is to change the soul."[67] What it meant in concrete terms was that neoliberal economic and public policies were not merely concerned with using market forces and rationality to efficiently allocate scarce resources in society. Rather, the goal was to create a new society by means of transforming the human soul. Consequently, in Africa under neoliberal economic policies, subsidies were eliminated and the food market was deregulated notwithstanding the fact that Western nations continue to subsidize their farmers. Even, if there were legitimate reasons for these reforms, they brought great suffering to the masses, for which reason the masses distrusted the government and withdrew from the public sphere to informal groups and associations.[68] It was, in fact, a case of the end justifying the means. Therefore, in the final analysis, postcolonial African nations now became primarily concerned with making their countries business-friendly in order to attract foreign investment and capital which would help them to develop and, presumably, to become strong competitors in the global economy. Subsequently, many sectors of the postcolonial economy, under neoliberal economic policies and conditions, canonized by the Washington Consensus, promoted free trade, financial liberalization, and deregulation.[69]

As expected, many African countries were ultimately forced to re-brand themselves economically as well as politically in a way that would enable them to attract clients, in this instance, foreign investors and tourists, a situation likened to immoral prostitution. Amazingly, that initiated a process that transformed the relationship between African countries and diaspora-based Black people and their leaders. Toward that end, African countries began to perceive Blacks in the diaspora in instrumental terms, especially as the priority now was for their countries in Year of Return to attract tourism, foreign investment, and greater home remittances in the form of migrant-dollars that was to presumably increase spending and stimulate further economic activities and growth. Unique African and national interests were sacrificed for the sake of business and the class interests of foreign investors and their local allies. In this set of circumstances, Nkrumah's brand of Pan-Africanism was forgotten for a while and, if heard about at all, it was in pursuit of commercial and business strategies. The movement now, however, did become *neoliberal* Pan-Africanism. Ghana with the best history of promoting Pan-Africanism became the first country to implement neoliberal economic policies (SAP). Justin Williams has summarized, in his 2016 published work, the fate of Pan-Africanism under the regime of neoliberal globalization in Africa in the following words:

> Because of the major paradigm shifts in Ghana's political culture initiated by the Rawlings regime, the spread of neoliberal policies across the continent, and the lack of progress made on regional integration, Pan-Africanism in Africa would have to be a project operating within the framework of explicitly capitalist economy moving forward. This is why Pan-Africanist engagement of African-Americans is largely based on the language of capital investment and consumption rather than anti-colonial revolutionary racial solidarity. Despite this being the antithesis of Nkrumah's vision in many ways, free market Pan-Africanism is proving to be an increasingly important and enduring aspect of Ghana's political culture of neoliberal democracy.[70]

The preceding quote, in essence, suggests that Pan-Africanism of today qualitatively means something different from the vision and spirit of Ghana's late president Kwame Nkrumah, one of the leading proponents of the movement. This is in spite of the fact that the AU adopted the New Partnership for African Development (NEPAD) as a developmental strategy in the 21st century to cope with the fast-paced rate of neoliberal globalization. Indeed, many critics have argued that NEPAD is neoliberalism dressed in African nationalist jargon, but in reality, it only provides opportunity for the developed and richer countries of the world with the solid capital and relative mastery of science, economic entrepreneurship, technology, and engineering easy entry into poorer countries where they could invest their money and extract high profits with very little regulation for the protection of the interests of the masses.[71] Most certainly, the African elites gain privately from such policies; therefore, Abdi Samatar (1950–) makes it very clear that he has nothing against what others see as Chinese exploitation of Africa in the 21st century, indeed at a time when nations of the AU seem to lack qualified construction engineers (or so it seems) who could have helped in building the AU's official secretariat in Addis Ababa, which was built and donated by the Chinese as a gift to Africa. Samatar further has the following to say about his reflection on this serious issue of concern:

"The PRC did not invite others to China to build such things as domes of shame, but instead ensured that its people learned to build and develop enterprises by doing it the old-fashioned way. Chinese companies that are building infrastructure in Africa developed through such processes. Unfortunately, in Africa, the state elite prefer to have others build world class structures for them as they do not trust that their people can learn to do so. . . . Travelling around the continent, one readily sees all types of construction, such as highways, railways, hydroelectric dams, theatres, government buildings, etc., being built by Chinese public and private companies. In such sites, one easily observes that Africans employed in these projects are labourers. All the technical operations are carried out by Chinese and in some cases, even the labourers come from China. . . . The ultimate antidote to the "Dome of Shame" is the development of African public and private enterprises that can nurture skilled and talented workforce which will create vibrant economies that can sustain decent livelihood. If African governments allow their people to learn by doing, I am confident that Africans will build their monuments of glory."[72]

The foregoing Samatar reflection highlights the serious failure of postcolonial African development to empower African citizens so they could be proud to be indigenes of the continent. One way this manifests itself and blossoms into a crisis in the making is the manner in which African countries seriously neglect their younger generation.

PAN-AFRICANISM AND THE YOUNGER (OR "WAITHOOD") GENERATION

One issue that runs with full speed throughout the history of Pan-Africanism is the vision and struggle of the movement since its emergence was sustained and regenerated through the works and efforts of successive younger generations. For instance, the generation that shifted Pan-Africanism to a focus on Africa after the 1945 Pan-African Congress in Manchester involved many young African students and professionals. One is of the assumption that the movement will thrive and flourish in Africa. However, one doubts the role and place of the current generation of African youth in the promotion of the vision of leaders of the past. The doubt stems from the fact that contemporary Africa lacks an effective mechanism for the integration of the youth into productive roles in the public sphere. Indeed, the great majority of African youth are now categorized as belonging to the so-called *waithood* or younger generation.[73] In essence, "waithood" in Africa today is described in literature as the period of living in suspension between childhood and adulthood. It is a prolong period of adolescence; an involuntary situation that delays one from moving to full adult status. At the basic level, the situation of "waithood" adversely affects the ability of the youth to do so many relevant things. For example, they are unable to secure jobs and, above all, lack the opportunities to be involved in meaningful, ennobling, appropriate, and effective living. Consequently, they are unable to pay their bills, live independently, and take care of themselves.

Due to the semblance of youth incapacitation, the African youth cannot even raise a family of their own, let alone provide the protection and support that a family deserves. Many of the youngsters have joined violent religious and criminal groups. As a result of all these complex challenges and problems, the youth cannot cultivate, nor fully engage in civic responsibilities. All the foregoing problems affect the youth and the imagination of Africa's people because they continue to live in the continuous present, which makes it hard to plan for the future. It is in this respect that the phenomenon of "waithood" generation makes the pursuit of Pan-African ideals by youngsters far-fetched because the struggle for basic survival leaves little time for the pursuit of higher-order needs in the context of Pan-African ideals by these youths.

Specifically, while the youth in Tunisia and Egypt played a very important role in removing the dictators, who led their countries for decades, one can surmise that while such struggles were admirable, their action cannot be said to fall within the realm of Pan-Africanism. They were simply struggling about local and national issues of concern. In other words, the issues which prompted the spring uprisings were critical to the Egyptian and Tunisian Arab youths. Consequently, the uprisings cannot be translated continentally into issues with Pan-African leanings.

PAN-AFRICANISM AND RELIGION

Where religion or religious fervor is concerned, an assertion that comes to mind instantly has much to do with the interpretation by the Black Power Movement of Stokely Carmichael (who renamed himself as Kwame Ture; 1941–1998). The memorable quotation is in the following words: "Pan-Africanism is the highest political expression of black power. It means one country, one government, one leader, one army, and this government will protect Africans all over the world whenever they face racial discrimination and economic exploitation."[74] Starting from this premise, Pan-Africanism today has the burden of wrestling with its diminished relevance and significance vis-à-vis religious sectarianism and parochial consciousness. Such an observation is relevant and pertinent because as many postcolonial leaders felt a lot more insecure, they became overly concerned about protecting colonial borders and boundaries of nation-states created by colonial rulers to promote their domination. However, in addition to the divisive role of ethnicity prevalent in contemporary Africa, many people have greater loyalty to and a strong sense of identity with their religion and their sect in particular, vis-à-vis the nation, showing little or no concern for Pan-Africanist thought.[75]

In fact, it is undeniable that many Africans have lost trust in the postcolonial state, which presumably was very concrete and palpable compared to the ideas of Pan-Africanism. For many ordinary citizens, who never received Western education or serious mobilization, Pan-Africanism is an abstract and, indeed, an elitist ideal and agenda. In their perception, it was in order to monopolize power and entrench themselves that many postcolonial African elites demobilized the citizenry with no plan for "conscientizing" such citizens the way Burkina Faso's assassinated President Sankara did, for he encouraged the citizens to be part of the nation-building project, the pathway to Pan-Africanism.[76] With the failure of the postcolonial state in most African countries to perform its promised official roles, many nations became virtually irrelevant to the lives of many people. Indeed, in some cases, the state authorities became nuisances as they engaged in predatory acts rather than being tools for development. It is in this constricted social condition and situation that many Africans sought primary identity, refuge, and shelter away from the central government and instead found solace in the religious and spiritual realm.

Islamic fundamentalism and violent jihad, for example, have created serious disruptions in many African countries, such as Kenya and Somalia. In Egypt, the primary concern of the Muslim Brotherhood, in supporting former president Morsi (1951–2019), was to create an ideal Islamic state and republic.[77] Members of the Brotherhood did not have a vision that was inclusive of all Egyptians, let alone a commitment to Pan-Africanism. This effort to create an Islamic revival and Muslim community with claims to exclusive access to truth is equally countered by the rapid spread of Pentecostal Christianity across many countries in Africa. Just as there are Muslim fundamentalists who claim to have exclusive access to truth and are committed to creating an Islamic communal utopia, there are Pentecostal Christians whose vision of identity and citizenship is limited to Christocentric righteousness as they define it.[78]

Meanwhile, across many African countries such radical Muslims call non-adherents to their brand of Islam "infidels," while the Christians on their part call the Muslims, "unbelievers," "the lost," "people living in darkness." Sometimes, terms such as "gentiles" and "heathen" are used as descriptors. Surely, this kind of sentiment or disposition is not congruent with the spirit and vision of Pan-Africanism advocated by leaders like the late president Nkrumah and his allies, an issue that underscored a sense of shared solidarity and a cosmopolitan sense of belonging across the continent.

In fact, religion—as it is currently practiced—has become a major threat to Pan-Africanism, apart from its parochial vision of human identity. It promotes an enchanted vision of the world.[79] Most certainly, a strongly enchanted vision of the world is not inherently wrong, yet it is not consistent with a modern society that is based on reason, rationality, progress, and the use of modern technology. Of course, African countries have the legitimate right to lead a pre-industrial life, whereby peace and tranquility presumably satiate the tranquil nausea of a bucolic state of being. Conversely, it is obvious that many religious people are not inspired by their faith to derive systematic solutions to social problems and challenges of development that are faced by Africa. For example, West African countries had to rely on the intervention of the global community through medical science instead of a miracle and prayer for an effective solution to the Ebola virus pandemic, which killed many people in Liberia, Guinea, and Sierra Leone, due partly to ignorance. Increasingly, it is also a documented fact that many Africans believe that God's miraculous intervention is the only hope for the future of their respective nations and the continent as a whole.[80] Their religious faith discourages them from exerting their energy in search of rational and scientific solutions to problems such as communicable diseases, the eradication or alleviation of poverty, including significant progress on the issue of gender inequality and injustice condoned by religious canons and cultural injunctions.

The reason why this kind of religion is incongruent with Pan-Africanism is because advocates of the movement desire African countries to stand on their own among the comity of nations. However, doing so will require having a solid and autonomous capacity to understand and utilize modern science and technology for national development and relative economic independence. Yet, there is an unfortunate situation where foreign and colonial influences shape both fundamentalist Islam and Pentecostal Christianity in Africa.[81] While all the preceding discussion may create a sense of depression and melancholy about the state of Pan-Africanism today, where the African continent is concerned, the election of former Senator Barak Hussein Obama as the president of the United States, the most powerful country in the world, did rejuvenate a sense of hope and efficacy among Black people in and outside Africa and among all persons considered as downtrodden and underdogs.

PAN-AFRICANISM OVERSEAS: IN THE OBAMA ERA

Pan-Africanism, during the Ghana regime of the late president Nkrumah and his generation of Africa leaders, became domiciled in Africa, especially with the formation of the OAU, now known as the AU. As a matter of fact, the original inspiration that galvanized participation in the movement started in the diaspora. Along the same pattern, as Black identity and experience suffered humiliation in both Africa and the diaspora, former Illinois Senator Obama's election did galvanize sentiment that reinvigorated a sense of Pan-Africanism.[82] As he titled his biography *The Audacity of Hope*, former president Obama's election victory created a sense of hope and pride among all Black people and among all progressive forces. The essence is well captured by Dr. Zeleza, in the following words, with reference to Pan-Africanism:

> The rise of Obama, just like the demise of colonialism and apartheid, whatever their subsequent limitations, were products of protracted struggles. It is in this sense that Obama is a powerful symbol for the Pan-African world. He is a symbol of black cognitive and cultural capacities for so long dismissed and derided by whites. He serves as the signified and signifier of black citizenship and African globality, who projects a new image of the African arrival and presence in America. As the son of a transient Kenyan immigrant, not a descendant of the historic diaspora, Obama reconnects the old diaspora to Africa and vice-versa in more immediate, intimate, and innovative ways. His persona and trajectory simultaneously reaffirm and reconfigure Pan-African connections, and shatter the insidious narratives of rupture proclaimed so loudly in Paul Gilroy's *Black Atlantic* and Keith Richburg's *Out of America*.[83]

Most certainly, it was an undeniable fact that the Black people of the world and all progressive forces were surely energized by President Obama's election. However, on another note, just as Obama's election regenerated a sense of hope and pride for Pan-Africanism as Zeleza has explained above, the historical event also exemplified the tension between a focus on personality on the one hand and on the other a focus on social structural factors vis-à-vis the effort to account for the forces that shape history and initiate social transformation.[84]

It was very clear that former president Obama had good intentions for meaningful social transformation in the United States and the world. Yet, structural constraints inherent in the American society as well as the political economy and the institutional structure of the global community frustrated his efforts. These impediments left him an American president pure and simple, for he was only able to pursue matters of interest to American national interest at all cost. Had Obama not done so, he would not have been re-elected.[85] Of course, if American national interest was the same as that of all other people and nations, Obama's actions would not be an issue of concern. Similarly, in the era of neoliberal globalization, there is no guarantee that all African nations regard their national interests as synonymous with those of the ruling elites as well as the ordinary citizens.[86] Indeed, what we have is at best neoliberal Pan-Africanism, which is a cause for lamentation.

CRITICAL INTERROGATION: A CONCLUSION

It is part of our critical interrogation as well as re-interpretation of Pan-Africanism, when we scrutinize the ideology in a constructive way in consonance with the realities of the 21st century, a "Big Brother is Watching You" period of George Orwellian parlance. Therefore, one may, initially, be tempted to disagree with the naiveté of some well-meaning and well-intentioned Pan-Africanists, who simply assume that—for Pan-Africanism to have a solid tap-root existence—there is the need to imbibe a specific foundational belief in pre-colonial African unanimity of culture and personality. Indeed, if one assumes that this oneness of culture existed, one can still legitimately query the validity of this claim in view of all the social and historical changes that Africa has gone through, wondering if such a romanticized African past can fully be retrievable today.

On another note, scholars — who have broadly read European intellectual history — should be in a position to realize that, in spite of what appears as unified European identity and thought, the literature on philosophical nationalism known as German Idealism did demonstrate that Germans did see themselves as different from the French. That was particularly the case when they reacted to the ideology and events that unfolded during the 1789 French Revolution. This much is well articulated in the works of Johann Herder and Johann Fichte.[87]

On the anthropological plane, human identity evolves in spite of the existence of the European Union today; this does not mean that European national cultures have nothing unique about them. Many European nations possessed a strong national identity up to the beginning of the 20th century. The key issue is that what Europeans want for themselves and how they plan to reconstruct their identity and social reality to achieve those goals. This is the same kind of concern and challenge that Pan-Africanists need to address in Africa instead of trying to diminish the uniqueness of different cultures and peoples. Within the broad family of the human race, there is unity in diversity.

Then, on a similar note, in the realm of Pan-Africanism, there is need for a critical as well as constructive interrogation and critique of a brand of African studies referred to as Afrocentrism. This is particularly so if Africans are to inculcate a sense of proportion and calmness in their reaction to issues of Eurocentrism. Since intellectual history shows that European identity is not as coherent as subsumed, there is no reason to insist that the legitimacy of African concerns can only be justified with some exclusively African experience, as if every group in the world should focus on its own "centrism" as the basis of intellectual engagement!

Furthermore, it has been the interesting conclusion of some scholars that a careful reading of European history would reveal that all European scholarship and their intellectuals have the same vision, and that they pursued that vision lockstep with one another. This is false, as numerous European scholars have condemned injustice against other European people in their writings and have engaged world history with a high level of human inclusiveness and a cosmopolitan mindset.[88] For example, in the European context, Edmund Burke was considered one of the founding fathers of conservative tradition in Britain, but he condemned British colonial rule in India because of its destruction of Indian culture and heritage.[89] Karl Marx certainly perceived British colonial rule in India as progressive in terms of transforming the mode of production, while acknowledging the violence that the colonial experience entailed.[90] Marx equally ridiculed European peasants as being a "sack of potatoes." Although the comment is regrettable, his critique was not racial in its spirit but theoretically inspired. Ghana's former president Nkrumah, a leading Pan-Africanist, was, during his college days in the United States, very significantly influenced by Marxist and Hegelian vision of history. He, however, reinterpreted and re-conceptualized their theoretical analysis to fit his mission and context. Not surprisingly, Marx was a European, but he did not write in favor of the European ruling and bourgeois classes. Rather, he wrote in favor of the oppressed classes all over the world. Therefore, it seems obvious that African scholars should borrow from Nkrumah by revisiting and contextualizing and re-conceptualizing what has been read to cohere with their social context. We hold the view that African scholars need to be constantly ready to adopt and adapt ideas relevant to their own needs from any part of the world instead of withdrawing into the Afrocentric intellectual cocoon.

Third, in his previously quoted writings, Zeleza has progressively highlighted the fact that President Obama's election was a great source of rejuvenation of Pan-African pride and cultural efficacy an indication that the continent's citizens possess the capacity to succeed like other races. However, as a follow up to an earlier point, former Illinois Senator Obama could not have won the American presidential election by using Afrocentrism as his rallying/clarion call. Rather he developed a political platform and vision that was inclusive of other American racial groups, convincing them to vote for him in spite of his African ancestry. It is worthy to note that many people who supported and voted for Barak Obama either did not vote at all or failed to vote for Mrs. Hillary Clinton in the 2016 presidential elections. Furthermore, it is also a fact that many Pan-Africanists outside the United States had no voting power, yet still had great sympathy for the Obama candidacy and, in their own way, actively gave him moral support. Therefore, it is an undeniable fact that in the 21st century Afrocentrism must be subsumed under a broad vision identifiable by all humanity irrespective of racial identity and geographical location, or else issues discussed under this theme would be considered only part of a local agenda.

On the Pan-Africanist plane, it is important to underscore the fact that when Africa's future challenges and opportunities are properly conceptualized and disseminated as part of a broad struggle for human dignity, many people—who have no historical, genealogical, or ancestral connection to Africa—can still commit their support to strategies which emanate from its ideals. It is a truism that the contributions by some Western scholars and professionals to Africa's development and in the promotion of a sense of equality of Africans with other racial groups is far more impressive than the efforts of predatory African elites who have done great damage to Africa's future, giving the terrible quagmire the African continent finds itself. It is this situation that has prompted Rene Dumont (1904–2001), a French sociological scholar, to write his seminal monograph *False Start in Africa*, arguing that the continent's march toward decolonization was a false pretense. There is a need for Africanists to inquire as to whether their strategy for elevating the human dignity of Africans should be uniquely tied to pre-industrial traditions or be part of the shared humanity of the whole human race!

Fourth, many of those with the awareness of Pan-Africanism often celebrated the need for decolonization from Western colonialism and imperialism as well as the internal oppression by the postcolonial political leadership class. Yet, they forget that at the core of colonial domination is *libido dominandi* (i.e., the lust to conquer and dominate), which is rooted in the inequality of power and privilege. That is why the ideal of Pan-Africanism should be to conquer all aspects of Eurocentrism. However, Africans should be careful against internal colonialism and, as mentioned earlier, oppression within all African countries as well as between ethnic and religious groups. This admonition stems from the lessons learned in Liberia, when Americo-Liberians (as emancipated slaves) meted out treatment that bordered on dehumanization and outright oppression of the natives they encountered. Their motto, crafted in the coat of arms of Liberia, reads "Love of liberty" the reason for settling in Liberia. However, their disregard for the natives of this West African nation caused the indigenous Liberian leadership to create an opposing slogan which harped on the notion that "Love of liberty met them in Liberia." That is why it is incumbent for true Pan-Africanists to issue a clarion call urging people in Africa to simultaneously fight against European neocolonialism and imperialism as well as internal colonialism among themselves.

Fifth, on another note, a constructive critical approach to Pan-Africanism must transcend and systematically reject neoliberal Pan-Africanism, which merely subscribes to the frame of African unity and identity while promoting growth without development. Although, many African countries, since decolonization, have experienced an impressive rate of economic growth, poverty reduction is not as impressive as expected. That is why many Africans are unfortunately labeled as "surplus people" in the strict economic sense, mainly because they lack the marketable skills or the human capital relevant to the neoliberal global economy and market. Furthermore, they neither have effective purchasing power to compel businesses to plead for their patronage nor produce any commodity that is of value to the global economy. Many of them do not make up to $1.50 per day, while the European Union under the common agricultural policy subsidizes the cows of every farmer at not less than $2.50 per day.[91] In Pan-African parlance, what this means statistically is that even in the 21st century it is proverbially better to be a cow in Europe than a human being in Africa with no production power. It is on this basis that many Africans wonder if Pan-Africanists should not contemplate ways of assisting in establishing a solid foundation for human dignity among Africans as part of the long-term goal of realizing the ideals of the movement.

On a final note, one may either deduce or conclude that the ideals of Pan-Africanism will have no future on the African continent if the youths are ignored and left to struggle on their own. After all, it is a fact of life that no society or movement can sustain itself without effectively and concretely integrating its youthful population. Furthermore, Pan-Africanism will be seen in hypocritical terms if its adherents fail to concretely and seriously address known issues of gender inequality in numerous spheres of public life. Although the problem of gender inequality is not exclusively an African problem, in many African countries, the struggle for gender equality is behind the curve. Similarly, women are behind their male counterparts at work when it comes to salaries and wages because of the lack of equity. Additionally, some African men use their power and privilege to dominate the womenfolk, relying on the canons of religion, cultural stereotypes, and biological differences between the sexes as explanations and justifications for denying women full human dignity and rights. Colonial rulers used similar cultural and religious and biological arguments to justify the racial inferiority of all colonized people irrespective of gender.[92] However, many Pan-Africanists—nationalists and radical scholars—appropriately fought against the colonialist from varied fronts on that score, emphasizing the need for dignity, equality, and justice for all humankind. For such Pan-Africanists, it is simply lamentable hypocrisy to condone and justify gender inequality in postcolonial Africa on dubious and morally duplicitous grounds! Furthermore, for Pan-Africanism to be seen in enduring and progressive terms, its proponents as well as ardent adherents should, in the final analysis, make it an inclusive organization (or movement) for all and sundry in Africa and in the Black diaspora.[93]

Chapter 3

PAN-AFRICANISM, AFRO-ASIAN SOLIDARITY, AND THE NON-ALIGNED MOVEMENT AND VISIBLE CHALLENGES

An interesting perspective is that nations subscribing to Pan-Africanism also became very involved in the promotion of the Non-Aligned Movement in Southeast Asia spearheaded by Indonesia under Sukarno, whose radical government would suffer a military overthrow similar to what Nkrumah (Ghana), Modibo Keita (Mali), and others had suffered. In fact, the University of South Africa's Development Studies Professor Sabelo J. Ndlovu-Gatsheni in *Empire, Global Coloniality And African Subjectivity* (2013) pointed out that, in the international context, "Pan-Africanism is rooted in struggles against the racial hierarchies of the international system that encouraged the slave trade."[94]

Ndlovu-Gatsheni further pointed out that the well-known "slave revolts in the so-called 'New World' and the literary works produced in the 'slave triangle' indirectly laid the foundation for Pan-Africanism."[95] That was prior to the time when West Indian–born Henry Sylvester Williams, a lawyer by training, formed the African Association in London in 1897 to boost Pan-African unity among all nations within the British Empire at the time. Subsequently, Williams would go ahead to organize "the first international Pan-African Congress in 1900."[96] Most certainly, the importance of that maiden Congress marked the first time that, in fact, Black people who had suffered extreme racism had met in a colonial capital to discuss relevant Pan-African issues. An important document that was drafted at the Congress by Dr. W.E.B. DuBois for dissemination was titled "To the nations of the World." Pan-Africanists were, indeed, very proud of their movement, which they saw as a redemptive project embodying ideals of freedom from such evils as slavery, racism, colonialism inequality, disunity, and exploitation on the African continent; also, Pan-Africanism, as experts have concluded, "rose not only as part of humankind's quest for liberty, freedom, justice and liberation but also as a direct response to the historical reality of enslavement of black races."[97]

At this point, leading African leaders showed divisiveness, "which symbolized a divided house that was destined to collapse under the weight of neo-colonial forces."[98] The establishment of the OAU in May 1963, with Diallo Telli, Guinea's former United Nations Ambassador, as its first secretary-general, became a reality "despite divisions among African leaders over what kind of union was to be formed."[99] As a pioneering African leader, Nkrumah, according to observers at the 1963 founding conference, "wanted the establishment of an African Union Government straightaway to lay the foundations of a United States of Africa."[100]

Nkrumah's efforts impressed his fellow African leaders a great deal although he could not unite the divided African house. However, he added to his clarion calls for such unity in the 1963 publication of the book[101] *Africa Must Unite*. Thematically, he wrote in the book about what neocolonialism could do, adding that African leaders needed "the strength of our combined numbers as a resource to protect ourselves from the very positive dangers of returning colonialism in disguised forms." In fact, Nkrumah and Nyerere posed challenges of varying degrees. To many, he was relatively the realist and pragmatist compared to Nkrumah, who wanted unity immediately and at any cost. While Nkrumah too was seen as an Afro-positivism, Nyerere was labeled an Afro-pessimist. It was, therefore, not surprising that Nyerere, contrary to Nkrumah's radical suggestions for unity, proposed: "To rule out a step-by-step progress towards African Unity, is to hope that the Almighty will one day say, 'Let there be unity in Africa,' and there shall be unity."[102]

Even though Nyerere and Nkrumah had a lot in common, especially where African socialism was concerned, he was seen at the 1963 founding conference to have tried to dampen the spirit of the Ghanaian leader. Yet, at the 1965 OAU Conference in Cairo, Egypt, he urged "his fellow African leaders to realize that the political and economic crisis bedeviling Africa were a clear testimony of the dangers of neocolonialism to Pan-African unity."[103] In the annals of the Non-Aligned movement, for example, there was the coming together of the like-minded as well as the drawing together of nations with a common identity and history of colonialism-*cum*-imperialism. They were countries that gathered at the April 1955 Bandung conference, which marked the maiden movement for African and Asian countries to raise the flag of solidarity. Transparently, as June Milne wrote in *Panaf Great Lives: Sekou Toure* (1978): "These were for the most part the people of former colonies and the smaller states, who had for centuries been deprived of meaningful voices in world affairs, and were determined not to be drawn into cold war politics."[104] That was at the maiden Afro-Asian Solidarity Conference, the second of which was held in Conakry, Guinea, in April 1960. At both events, Pan-Africanism played a transparent role and, in that year, it was affirmed by Nkrumah, Nasser, Toure and other radical leaders as part of the way forward for the Black race.

NOTES

1. Harcourt Fuller. 2014. *Building The Ghanaian Nation-State: Kwame Nkrumah's Symbolic Nationalism*. New York: Palgrave-Macmillan.
2. Ibid. p. xvii.

3. Ghana's late President Kwame Nkrumah made the quoted declaration on January 7, 1961 at the annual conference of the then OAU, now called the African Union (AU) in Casablanca, Morocco.

4. Abdul Karim Bangura. 2019. *Falolaism: The Epistemologies and Methodologies of Africana Knowledge*. Durham, NC: Carolina Academic Press.

5. Ibid., p. 183.

6. Ibid. p. 4.

7. Ernest Harsch. 2015. "Thomas Sankara" in *African Leaders of the Twentieth Century*. Athens, OH: Ohio University Press, p. 151.

8. Ibid., p. 151.

9. Jeffrey S. Ahlman, 2017. *Living With Nkrumahism: Nation State and Pan-Africanism in Ghana*. Ohio University Press.

10. Napier, Diane Brook. 2013. "Pan-Africanism." In *Encyclopedia of Race and Racism*, 2nd ed., edited by Patrick L. Mason, 291–294. Vol. 3. Detroit: Macmillan Reference USA. *Gale Virtual Reference Library* (accessed May 1, 2017).

11. Esedebe P. Olisanwuche. 1994. *Pan-Africanism: The Idea and Movement, 1776–1991*. Washington, DC: Howard University Press.

12. "Pan-Africanism." 2016. In *The Columbia Electronic Encyclopedia (6th Edition)* by Paul Lagasse and Columbia University, Columbia University Press.

13. Thomas Hobbes. 2016. *Leviathan*. Penguin Books.

14. Michael Crowder. 1984. *West Africa Under Colonial Rule*. London: Hutchinson University Library for Africa. Readers may as well read more on the subject from A.B. Assensoh and Yvette M. Alex-Assensoh. 2016. *Malcolm X And Africa*. New York: Cambria Press, as well as in Kwame Nkrumah. 1964. *Neo-Colonialism: The Last Stage of Imperialism*. London: Panaf Books.

15. Olisanwuche, op. cit.

16. Ibid. Also see, The Female King of Colonial Nigeria: Ahebi Ugbabe in which Michigan State University History Professor Nwando Achebe discusses colonial Nigeria's female King Ahebi Ugbabe that among elite black female radical leaders, who can qualify in Pan-African leadership terms, are Funmilayo Ransome-Kuti (West Africa), Mamphela Ramphedele (southern Africa); Wambui Otieno (East Africa), Adelaide Smith Casely-Hayford (West Africa), Nelson Mandela (southern Africa) and others.

17. Bangura, op. cit, p. 458.

18. Justin Williams. 2016. *Pan-Africanism in Ghana: African Socialism, Neoliberalism, and Globalization*. Durham, NC: Carolina Academic Press. In *Malcolm X: A Biography* (2014), Professors A.B. Assensoh and Yvette M. Alex-Assensoh have discussed some of the moves that Malcolm X made, before his in 1965, to get the Cairo conference of the OAU to censure the USA for years of systemic discrimination and oppression of his fellow Blacks; he tried earlier to do so before the U.N. without success. To him, he was acting in the interests of Pan-Africanism.

19. Paul Tiyambe Zeleza. 2009. *Barack Obama and African Diasporas Dialogues and Dissensions*. Athens, OH: Ohio University Press; Paul Tiyambe Zeleza. 2011. "Pan-Africanism in the Age of Obama: Challenges and Prospects." *The Black*

Scholar 41(2): 34–44. Accessed May 1, 2017. Taylor and Francis Online. Yet, as Kwame Nkrumah has argued in some of his publications, its scientific strata, Pan-Africanism—just like socialism—does not need to have the varied strands that Dr. Zeleza has discussed but, like all intellectual exercise, each theorist is entitled to his or her opinions.

20. Zeleza, 2011, op. cit.
21. Williams, op. cit., p. 9. A very useful published monograph about freed slaves from America, who moved to Liberia, in the context of early Pan-Africanism in the 1830s is *Price of Liberty: African Americans and the Making of* Liberia (2004) by Claude A. Clegg III.
22. Martin R. Delany. 2003. "Principia of Ethnology: The Origin of Races and Color, with Archaeological Compendium of Ethiopian and Egyptian Civilizations from Years of Careful Examination and Inquiry." In *Martin R. Delany: A Documentary Reader*, edited by Robert S. Levine, 483. Chapel Hill, NC: University of North Carolina Press.
23. Owen Charles Mathurin. 1976. *Henry Sylvester Williams and the origins of the pan-African movement: 1869–1911.* Westport, CT: Greenwood, p. 68.
24. Brent Hayes Edwards. 2003. *The Practice of Diaspora: Literature, Translation and the Rise of Black Nationalism.* Cambridge, MA: Harvard University Press, p. 3.
25. Tyler Stovall. 2012. *Paris Noir African Americans in the City of Light.* Boston, MA: Houghton Mifflin.
26. Ibid.
27. Ibid.
28. Aime Cesaire. 1972. *Discourse on Colonialism.* New York: Monthly Review Press, p. 9
29. Paulin J. Hountondji. 2007. *African Philosophy: Myth and Reality.* Bloomington, IN: Indiana University Press.
30. Caroline Hutton and Robin Cohen. 1975. "African Peasants and Resistance to Change: A Reconsideration of Sociological Approaches." In *Beyond the Sociology of Development: Economy and Society in Latin America and Africa*, edited by Robin Cohen, Ivaar Oxaal, Tony Barnett, and David Booth, 105–130. New York: Routledge; Rayah Feldman. 1975. "Rural Social Differentiation and Political Goals in Tanzania." In *Beyond the Sociology of Development: Economy and Society in Latin America and Africa*, edited by Robin Cohen, Ivaar Oxaal, Tony Barnett, and David Booth, 154–182. New York: Routledge.
31. Paulin J. Hountondji. 2007. *African Philosophy: Myth and Reality.* Bloomington, IN: Indiana University Press.
32. Ali Al'Amin Mazrui, Ricardo René Laremont, and Tracia Leacock Seghatolislami. 2003. *Africanity Redefined.* Trenton, NJ: Africa World, pp. 99–116.
33. Seifudein Adem and Kimani Njogu. 2018. *Black Orwell: Essays on the Scholarship of Ali A. Mazrui.* Trenton, NJ, USA: Africa World Press.
34. Michael Crowder. 1984. *West Africa Under Colonial Rule.* London: Hutchinson University Library for Africa.
35. David Levering Lewis. 1993. *W. E. B. Du Bois - Biography of a Race: 1868–1919.* New York: Henry Holt and Company.

36. W. E. B. Du Bois. 1915. "The African Roots of the War," *The Atlantic Monthly*, pp. 707–714.
37. Colin Legum. 1977. *Pan-Africanism: A Short Political Guide*. London: Greenwood, p. 133.
38. Williams, op. cit., pp. 11–13.
39. Ibid., pp. 12–13.
40. Ibid.
41. Ibid., pp. 14–15.
42. Ibid.
43. Ibid, p. 16.
44. Ibid.
45. Kwame Nkrumah. 1972. *Ghana: the Autobiography of Kwame Nkrumah*. New York: International Publishers.
46. Williams, op. cit., p. 16.
47. Ibid, 17.
48. Olisanwuche, op. cit.
49. Hakim Adi. 1998. *West Africans in Britain: 1900–1960: Nationalism, Pan-Africanism, and Communism*. London: Lawrence and Wishart; Tajudeen Abdul-Raheem. 1996. *Pan Africanism: Politics, Economy and Social Change in the Twenty-first Century*. London: Pluto, p. 4.
50. Sherwood, Marika. 1996. *Kwame Nkrumah: The Years Abroad: 1935–1947*. Legon: Freedom Publ., p. 125.
51. Ibid.
52. A. B. Assensoh. 1989. *Kwame Nkrumah of Africa: His Formative Years and the Beginning of His Political Career, 1935–1948*. Elms Court: Arthur Stockwell Ltd.
53. Olisanwuche, op. cit., pp. 165–191.
54. Goran Hyden. 1985. *No Shortcuts to Progress: African Development Management in Perspective*. London: Heinemann. Rene Dumon's book, *False Start in Africa* is seen as a pioneering work to guide scholars of African independence.
55. Paulin J. Hountondji. 2007. *African Philosophy: Myth and Reality*. Bloomington, IN: Indiana University Press.
56. Hutton and Cohen, op. cit., pp. 105–130; Feldman, op. cit., 154–182.
57. Hamza Alavi. 1972. "The State in Postcolonial Societies: Pakistan and Bangladesh." *New Left Review* 1(74); Colin Leys. 1976. "The 'Overdeveloped' Postcolonial State: A Re-Evaluation." *Review of African Political Economy*, (5): 39–48.
58. Mahmood Mamdani. 1996. *Citizen and Subject: Contemporary Africa and the Legacy of Late Colonialism*. Princeton, NJ: Princeton University Press.
59. G. O. Olusanya. 1966. "The Zikist Movement-A Study in Political Radicalism, 1946-50." *The Journal of Modern African Studies* 4(3): 323–333.
60. David L. McKee and William H. Leahy. 1970. "Urbanization, Dualism and Disparities in Regional Economic Development." *Land Economics* 46(1): 82–85; Lipton, Michael. 1989. *Why Poor People Stay Poor: A Study of Urban Bias in World Development*. Aldershot: Avebury.

61. Richard Sandbrook. 2000. *The Politics of Africa's Economic Stagnation*. Cambridge: Cambridge University Press.

62. Naomi Chazan. 1999. *Politics and Society in Contemporary Africa*. Boulder, CO: Lynne Rienner Publishers.

63. Peter B. Evans. 1995. *Embedded Autonomy: States and Industrial Transformation*. Princeton: Princeton University Press, pp. 21–42.

64. Richard A. Joseph. 2014. *Democracy and Prebendal Politics in Nigeria: The Rise and Fall of the Second Republic*. Cambridge: Cambridge University Press.

65. J. Mensah. 2016. *Neoliberalism and Globalization in Africa: Contestations on the Embattled Continent*. New York: Palgrave-Macmillan.

66. Eric J. Evans. 2013. *Thatcher and Thatcherism*. London: Routledge. In Stuart Hall's 2017 published semi-memoir, *Familiar Stranger: A Life Between Two Islands*. Durham, NC: Duke University Press, readers have been informed about how Hall, who died in 2014, coined the term.

67. Catherine Kingfisher and Jeff Maskovsky. 2008. "The Limits of Neoliberalism." *Critique of Anthropology* 28(2): 119.

68. Donald Rothchild and Naomi Chazan. 1988. *The Precarious Balance State and Society in Africa*. Boulder, CO: Westview.

69. Dani Rodrik. 1996. "Understanding Economic Policy Reform." *Journal of Economic Literature* 34(1): 9.

70. Williams, op. cit., p. 113.

71. Ibid., pp. 115–136.

72. Abdi Ismail Samatar. "Africa's 'Dome of Shame' If African governments 'allow their people to learn by doing,' Africans will build their 'monuments of glory'." Aljazeera.com. December 7, 2012. Accessed May 2, 2017. http://www.aljazeera.com/indepth/opinion/2012/12/201212793126295253.html. Abdi Ismail Samatar is Professor of Geography at the University of Minnesota and a research fellow at the University of Pretoria, South Africa.

73. Alcinda Manuel Honwana. 2013. *The Time of Youth: Work, Social Change, and Politics in Africa*. Boulder, CO: Kumarian Press Pub.

74. Jonathan Power. 1971. "Carmichael Urges U.S. Blacks to Look to Africa." *New York Times*, February 6. Accessed May 2, 2017.

75. John F. McCauley. 2017. *The Logic of Ethnic and Religious Conflict in Africa*. Cambridge, UK: Cambridge University Press.

76. Ernest Harsch. 2014. *Thomas Sankara: An African Revolutionary*. Athens, OH: Ohio University Press.

77. Eric Trager. 2016. *Arab Fall: How the Muslim Brotherhood Won and Lost Egypt in 891 Days*. Washington, DC: Georgetown University Press.

78. Samuel Zalanga. 2010. "Religion, Economic Development and Cultural Change: The Contradictory Role of Pentecostal Christianity in Sub-Saharan Africa." *Journal of Third World Studies* 27(1): 43–62.

79. Paul Gifford. 2016. *Christianity, Development and Modernity in Africa*. New York: Oxford University Press.

80. Ibid.

81. Steven Brouwer, Paul Gifford, and Susan Rose. 1997. *Exporting the American Gospel: Global Christian fundamentalism*. London: Routledge.
82. Zeleza, 2009, op. cit.
83. Zeleza, 2011, op. cit.
84. Daron Acemoglu and James A. Robinson. 2013. *Why Nations Fail: The Origins of Power, Prosperity, and Poverty*. New York: Crown Business.
85. Charles A. Murray. 2013. *American Exceptionalism: An Experiment in History*. Washington, DC: AEI Press.
86. Mensah, op. cit.
87. Johann Gottlieb Fichte. 2013. *Addresses to the German Nation*. Indianapolis, IN: Hackett Publishing Company, Inc.; Johann Gottfried von Herder and T. O. Churchill. 1968. *Reflections on the Philosophy of the History of Mankind*. Chicago: University of Chicago Press.
88. James M. Blaut. 2000. *Eight Eurocentric Historians*. New York: Guilford Press; Eric R. Wolf. 2010. *Europe and the People Without History*. Berkeley, CA: University of California Press.
89. Jerry Z. Muller. 2011. *The Mind and the Market: Capitalism in Modern European Thought*. New York: Alfred A. Knopf, pp. 104–138.
90. Karl Marx, Friedrich Engels, and Robert C. Tucker. 1978. *The Marx-Engels Reader*. New York: Norton.
91. Larry Elliott. 2005. "Subsidizing Cows While Milking the Poor." *The Guardian*, October 17. Accessed May 2, 2017. https://www.theguardian.com/business/2005/oct/17/eu.internationalaidanddevelopment. Larry Elliott is economics editor of *The Guardian*.
92. J. Blaut. 2000. *Years of Activism Back in the Gold Coast, 1947–1957*. Guilford.
93. Sabelo J. Ndlovu-Gatsheni. 2013. *Empire, Global Coloniality and African Subjectivity*. New York: Berghahn Publishers, p. 60.
94. Ibid., 60.
95. Ibid., p. 60.
96. Ibid., p. 60.
97. Ibid., pp. 62–63.
98. Ibid., p. 64.
99. Ibid., p. 64.
100. Ibid., p. 64.
101. Ibid., p. 64.
102. Ibid., p. 64.
103. Ama Biney. 2008. "The Legacy of Kwame Nkrumah in Retrospect." *Journal of Pan-African Studies*, 16(3): 139. Ndlovu-Gatsheni, op. cit., pp. 66–67.
104. June Milne. 1978. *Panaf Great Lives: Sekou Toure*. London: Panaf Books, pp. 163–164.

Chapter 4

Years of Activism and Postcolonial Gold Coast, 1947–1960

By the fall of 1947, Nkrumah and his other Pan-African-minded African students, resident in various colonial capitals, including London and Paris, had concluded that it would continue to be difficult for them to fight colonialism and imperialism from overseas, instead of being on the African continent. With this in mind, Nkrumah accepted a one-way ticket to travel on a West Africa-bound ship, with the intention of going to the Gold Coast to serve as the secretary-general of the United Gold Coast Convention (UGCC) His memorable departure, accompanied by Kojo Botsio, his future foreign minister, took place on November 14, 1947, with plans to make brief stopovers in Liberia and in Sierra Leone, two English-speaking countries, which welcomed emancipated slaves.[1]

Nkrumah was well received by Dr. J.B. Danquah and all of the other UGCC leaders. Aside from monetary gifts and gifts of clothing, they also provided him with wise counsel. As Peter Omari spelled out in *Anatomy of an African Dictatorship* (1971), Nkrumah's arrival on the Gold Coast's political scene gave it a refreshed atmosphere, and created a true atmosphere of partisan politics due to his zeal as an organizer.[2]

Nkrumah did work hard for whatever he was being paid by the UGCC leaders, led by Dr. Danquah. In fact, within six months, Nkrumah had traveled far and wide to establish branches of the nationalist movement. Most of the branches were formed in some of the large towns in the Central and Western Regions, places with which he was very familiar before he left for further studies in America and, later, in the United Kingdom. His success in recruiting new members for the UGCC was also due to post-World War II frustrations of the indigenous peoples of the various African nations. Instead of working behind the scenes, the Gold Coast nationalist leaders, now spurred onto action by Nkrumah's hard work, decided to start speaking out about complete self-government which could lead to independence in colonial nations. With Nkrumah's organizational skills, the clarion call was: "Self-Government Now!"³

By December 1948, the British colonial authorities had plans to undermine Nkrumah's mass following. For a semblance of democracy, the British authorities, who had accused Nkrumah of being a socialist, seeking a so-called Union of West African Soviet Socialist Republics, decided to seek public opinion on what Nkrumah and his followers were trying to achieve: self-government. Therefore, a commission was established and headed by Sir Henley Coussey, a British Jurist. The report of the commission was in favor of the British colonial presence in the Gold Coast, a situation that hardened Nkrumah's resolve to find a way to lead his own anti-colonial mass movement.⁴

NKRUMAH'S DEPARTURE FROM UGCC AND FORMATION OF HIS NEW PARTY WITH CONTINENTAL UNITY IN MIND

Nkrumah felt that the UGCC leadership, made up mostly of professionals, did not appreciate his hard work for their Convention. That was why he decided to form and lead his own political party, the Convention People's Party (CPP). In his own words, the future president (Nkrumah), among other details, wrote: "On Sunday, 12th June, 1949, therefore, before an audience of about sixty thousand people, I announced the formation of the Convention people's Party [C.P.P.]."⁵

It was obvious that the UGCC leaders, who had blamed Nkrumah even for their previous arrests and detention by the British colonial administration, could not get along with Nkrumah, their general secretary. Therefore, breaking away from their organization was the logical thing to do. Nkrumah was correct in his estimation that if he did not take decisive actions with his new CPP organization, the colonial authorities would continue to control and oppress the Gold Coast and its people. That was clearly confirmed by the then British prime minister Winston Churchill, who said publicly: "I did not become the Prime Minister of His Majesty's Government in order to preside over the liquidation of the British Empire."⁶

At a mammoth rally, the crowd urged Nkrumah to resign from the UGCC and lead them in a new organization. He was told loudly: "Resign and lead us, and we shall complete the struggle together."⁷ At that juncture, Nkrumah was serious about making sure that the Gold Coast would not remain in the colonial ambit. Therefore, to ascertain that the anti-colonialist message reached every nook and corner of the colony, from where he was operating, he acquired motor vehicles and established newspapers, including *The*

Evening News of Accra, with the motto, "Forward ever, backward never." He confirmed these himself when he wrote: "Before long, we managed to collect together some motor vans to which we attached loudspeakers. These, together with the Accra Evening News, the Sekondi *Morning Telegraph*, and the Cape Coast *Daily Mail*, did yeoman service in broadcasting the propaganda of the party and in keeping alive the spirit of nationalism."[8]

Also, he made sure that even the youth of the colony were readied for the ongoing struggle; hence, established colleges and schools for them to receive more education. The colors of the new party's flag were red, white, and green.[9] When Nkrumah realized that the British colonial authorities were adamant about his quest for decolonization and self-governance of the Gold Coast, he decided to resort to other actions that the British authorities did not authorize. These included his plans to declare what he termed as "Positive Action," which was to be a constitutional and non-violent way of seeking independence for the Gold Coast. As a very clever politician, Nkrumah had explained at various meetings of indigenous groups: "I pointed out that there were two ways of achieving self-government, one by armed revolution, and the other by constitutional and legitimate non-violent methods."[10]

In preparing to declare "Positive Action," Nkrumah and his supporters were to make sure that British-made goods and allies of the colonial administration were boycotted. To make his stance clear, Nkrumah wrote on the front page of his *Evening News* newspaper what he described as "a stirring article headed 'The Era of Positive Action Draws Nigh.' Later, before a large gathering at the [Accra] Arena, I warned the people to prepare for Positive Action."[11] Fearing that Nkrumah was determined to arouse the people of the Gold Coast through his declaration of "Positive Action," the British colonial secretary wrote a stern letter to Nkrumah, which also contained an invitation for Nkrumah to meet the Colonial Secretary Sir R.H. Saloway, a former British civil servant working in the colonial administration in India, who was familiar with Mahatma Gandhi's non-violent civil disobedient tactics which helped India to attain its independence on August 15, 1947.[12]

At the subsequent meeting, the colonial secretary warned Nkrumah about his plans to instigate the public to resort to his so-called "Positive Action." In the end, the colonial administration decided to arrest leaders of Nkrumah's political party, but he was able to elude them initially so that he could assist those arrested. He recounted part of the order that his colleagues faced:

> Almost daily now, the police raided the party [CPP] Headquarters in an attempt to arrest as many of the leaders as they could round up. I just looked at them disinterestedly as they searched the place for I knew, as well as they did, that I was safe for the time being. I was to be their final kill.... On 17th January [1950] Kojo Botsio was arrested and detained at the police station, where I

managed to send food to him each day. As general secretary of the Party, his office was searched with tooth-comb thoroughness and all-party literature was confiscated.[13]

Toward the end of January 1950, the colonial authorities had made sure that all of Nkrumah's political allies had been arrested. It was on January 22, 1950, that he was to be arrested. So he reported casually, and when a police officer saw him, he rushed to arrest him, adding: "It seemed almost with apology that he took hold of my arm and as he informed me that I was under arrest."[14]

With Nkrumah under arrest, the colonial authorities built a strong criminal case against him, charging him with various offenses, including incitement as well as coercion of the colonial authorities to get freedom for the Gold Coast. In trying to be thorough with his judgment, the presiding magistrate, a European, explained to Nkrumah that since he was not a trade unionist, it was illegal for him to lead any strike or an industrial action. Nkrumah was ultimately convicted by the court and was given two sentences of 12 months each.[15] That, indeed, was not the end of his legal ordeal. Instead, he was driven from Accra to Cape Coast to be charged with sedition as publisher of the *Daily Mail* newspaper, which was a similar charge, for which editor Kofi Baako of the newspaper had been sent to prison earlier. Upon being convicted, Nkrumah received another 12-month sentence; added to the other 24 months, he had 36 months—or three years—to be served consecutively. He was imprisoned at James Fort Prison, which used to be a place for string enslaved Africans to be transferred to the Cape Coast castle for their journeys to the New World.[16]

The imprisonment was taken seriously by the colonial leaders of the Gold Coast. As it was with hard labor, Nkrumah and the other prisoners had to weave fishing nets. He, in particular, was not allowed to have any such writing tools as pen or paper for fear that he would communicate with his collaborators outside. Nkrumah was confident that his political party would do well in the forthcoming municipal elections because it had been well organized even though he was in jail. Surely enough, in the Accra municipal elections, six members of the CPP were elected; in other parts of the country, including Cape Coast, CPP candidates won the local municipal elections.[17]

Since Nkrumah's imprisonment was on a misdemeanor conviction but not a heinous crime, he was permitted to register and stand election in the forthcoming general elections. That was a gamble on the part of the colonial leaders, who thought that he would not do well. In order to encourage unity among the ethnic groups, Nkrumah decided to stand the election in Accra instead of his own Nzema area in the Western region of Ghana. In the 1951 general elections, which were a prelude to self-government, Nkrumah won his legislative assembly seat overwhelmingly: he received 22,780 votes out of the 23,122 total votes cast. The colonial authorities were so impressed with Nkrumah's performance in the general elections that they asked the prison superintendent to release him from the James Fort Prison on February 12, 1951, and that was done.[18] When coming out of the prison gates, Nkrumah's political allies, led by future finance minister K.A. Gbedemah, were outside waiting for him. The next day, on February 13, 1951, the freshly released prisoner, Nkrumah was to meet the colonial governor Sir Charles Noble Arden-Clarke. Nkrumah reported it this way:

> The day after my release from prison, I was invited by the Governor to meet him at nine o'clock that morning. When I walked into the courtyard of Christianborg Castle, the official residence of the Governor, I suddenly realized that it was the very first time I had set eyes on the place. The glaring white stone of the battlements, the impressive forecourt and the beauty of this imposing building with the roaring surf [of the sea] battering against its foundations, seemed to me like a new world. Although Sir Charles Arden-Clarke and I had been opposing each other for so many months past, I had no idea what he looked like, for we had never met. I wondered how I should be received. Had I known this man before, I should not have doubted the courtesy that would be shown to me.[19]

Nkrumah, in conveying his impression of the British colonial governor Sir Charles Arden-Clarke, added a description of how he looked like, and what immediately happened upon seeing the governor in his residence:

> A tall, broad-shouldered man, sun-tanned, with an expression of firmness and discipline but with a twinkle of kindness in his eyes came towards me with his hand stretched [to welcome me]; a hand that I noticed was large and capable looking. He welcomed me and asked me how I was. As we both sat down, I sensed that he must be feeling as alert and suspicious of me as I was of him. We lost little time, however, in coming down to the business at hand.[20]

In Nkrumah's further depiction of the encounter with the governor at his Christianborg Castle office, the soon-to-be indigenous people's leader reported that Sir Charles told him that, with the victory of his political party (the CPP) in the general elections, his Majesty's Government back in the United Kingdom was inviting him (Nkrumah) to form the first indigenous government to exercise internal leadership with him assuming the important title of Leader of Government Business. He was asked to select seven fellow citizens to serve as ministers in his indigenous cabinet. This he did for the following portfolios: Education/Social Welfare (Mr. Kojo Botsio); Health and Labor (Mr. K.A. Gbedemah); Agriculture and Natural Resources

(Mr. A. Casely-Hayford); Commerce, Industry, and Mines (Mr. T. Hutton-Mills); Communications and Works (Dr. Ansah Koi); Local Government (Mr. E.O. Asafu-Adjei); and Minister without Portfolio (Mr. J.A. Braimah).[21]

NKRUMAH AS LEADER OF GOVERNMENT BUSINESS; PRIME MINISTER, AND BEYOND, 1951–1957

As it has been previously noted, Nkrumah, instead, initially became Leader of Government Business. However, the indigenous population felt that Nkrumah was more than ready to head an independent Ghana. In fact, Kofi Buenor Hadjor, a distinguished Ghanaian writer, conveyed the correct sentiments of the people of the Gold Coast at the time when he pointed out that, for the people, the 1951 general elections should have been the election that would have given the country its independence with the first elected leader being Nkrumah. As far as Hadjor was concerned, the voters had made their choice known.[22] Nkrumah was very shortly surprised when almost exactly a year after serving as leader of Government Business, Governor Sir Charles Arden-Clarke in March 1952 announced publicly that Nkrumah was to be recognized as prime minister of the Gold Coast.[23]

For almost six years, Nkrumah and his CPP leadership ruled the Gold Coast until its full self-governance in 1957. It also meant that his political party held a majority in the new Legislative Council, which transformed to Ghana's national Parliament. Nkrumah wanted to make sure that the new ministers that he appointed understood the principles of his administration, especially as he told them in a meeting:

> There should be no fraternization, I said, between Assemblymen and European officials except on strictly official relations [or business]: for, what imperialists failed to achieve by strong-arm methods, they might hope to bring off with cocktail parties. I finally emphasized, however, that we were not fighting against race or color, but against a [colonial] system.[24]

However, Nkrumah did nothing to show either disrespect or ingratitude to the colonial governor whose duties included guiding Nkrumah and his new indigenous leadership to ensure a smooth transition to self-governance. Interestingly, however, the governor's appointees (R. H. Saloway, R. Amitage, and P. Branningan) exercised jurisdiction in all aspects of Defense, Law, Foreign Affairs, and Financial matters; that is, held the cabinet portfolios of ministers of defense, justice, foreign affairs, and finance; the appointees also became automatic ex-officio members of the 74-member legislative assembly. Those positions were considered so crucial for the smooth machinery of government that the governor reserved them for his home-trained British civil servants. There were also new physical offices assigned for the use of the new ministers. However, as Nkrumah disclosed later, after his initial appointment as Leader of Government Business (which changed in March 1952 to prime minister) "no provision had been made for an office for me, as if things had gone according to plan, the position would have been in the hands of the Attorney-General. Instead, I was given a room in the main ministry building near that of the Colonial Secretary."[25] Nkrumah, indeed, made sure that he and all of his new team of indigenous leaders performed well to demonstrate that they could very well govern the territory at independence. While governing at home, he also remembered his Pan-Africanist interests, including the fact that he had the wish to reunite in ideas and in deeds with the diaspora-based Black men and women he met in America, known as Negroes during the period. In keeping with his desire to reconnect with his friends, he accepted a 1951 invitation from his *alma mater* Lincoln University to serve as its commencement speaker and also to receive an honorary degree.

NKRUMAH RETURNS TO AMERICA

It was on May 30, 1951, barely six years after he had left America for good, that he and Mr. Kojo Botsio (1916–2001), his minister of education and social welfare, left the Gold Coast on their way back to America, through the colonial capital of London. Nkrumah and Mr. Botsio were in London for two days, and then departed for the United States. Upon their arrival in New York, they saw several people waiting to welcome them. Nkrumah was surprised, and he said so to Mr. Botsio, who was visiting America for the first time. Among those meeting Nkrumah was a U.S. State Department's protocol officer, as well as a delegation from Lincoln University, which included the late Lincoln University president Horace Mann Bond (1904–1972) and the Dean and leaders of the Lincoln University Alumni Association. Indeed, Nkrumah was thrilled by the treatment he received during his revisit to America. Looking at the enthusiastic welcome, Nkrumah expressed openly: "I felt honored indeed."[26]

A further honor that both Nkrumah and Botsio received was the fact that when leaving the New York Airport—John F. Kennedy or JFK airport—they had a police escort:

> With flash bulbs bursting on all sides, we were ushered into a car and driven to our hotel with a police escort. On arrival at the hotel, I held a press conference. I explained to the [news] reporters that my visit was of a dual purpose; that I was

there not only to receive an honorary degree from my old university but, also, I was anxious to explore avenues in the United States for obtaining technical assistance for the development of my country[27] [the Gold Coast].[28]

Most certainly, the honors for Nkrumah and Mr. Botsio continued because, as he wrote, they traveled from New York to Philadelphia, the capital of Pennsylvania, on their way to Lincoln University. In the city, the Mayor welcomed Nkrumah and Nkrumah reported that the Mayor presented him with the ceremonial key to the city. A place had been reserved for him and Botsio at the Bellevue-Stratford Hotel. At the hotel, America's World Affairs Council along with the Trustees of Lincoln University had arranged a joint luncheon in Nkrumah's honor. Both Nkrumah and Mr. Botsio spoke at the luncheon. On Nkrumah's part, he simply made sure that he told the audience about his struggle back in the Gold Coast and his victories at the polls. He also continued his appeal for British and American technicians to help build his young country.[29]

After the luncheon, Nkrumah asked to be taken to visit Temple University's Philatelic Museum. He let it be known that he thoroughly enjoyed the visit because, apart from his interest in philately, he also had a strong passion for museums of any kind. After much merrymaking, Nkrumah returned to his hotel room in Philadelphia to find out that en route from New York to Pennsylvania he had lost his suitcase. He added: "I checked with Kojo [Botsio] to see whether it had found its way to his [hotel] room by mistake, and then got in touch with the hotel porter. But nobody had seen my suitcase. My friends light-heartedly suggested that my belonging might have been taken for inspection by the Federal Bureau of Investigations [FBI], but whatever the reason, it was certainly inconvenient at the time."[30]

NKRUMAH'S APPEAL TO AFRICAN AMERICAN FRIENDS TO ASSIST THE GOLD COAST

During the June 1951 commencement, the then-Lincoln University president Bond, father of the late civil rights activist Julian Bond (1940–2015), introduced Ghana's future president Nkrumah, who was preparing to give the address that he had freshly prepared because the original one had been lost in his missing suitcase. He commented on it this way: "I had to have a few minutes in which to prepare my Commencement Address for the following day, and so I quietly escaped to my room in the hotel to write this. When I had finished [my first draft], I gave it to Kojo [Botsio] to read through and give his comments."[31] At the 1951 Lincoln University Commencement, Nkrumah was awarded the Doctor of Laws (LL.D.) honorary degree, a similar degree that, in 1962, his Lincoln contemporary and foreign minister of Ghana, Lawyer Ako Adjei (1916–2002) also received in 1962 from his own American *alma mater*. Nkrumah reported excitedly: "The President, Dr. Bond, conferred upon me the degree of Doctor of Laws, and I was invited to speak."[32]

The major part of Nkrumah's Commencement Address dealt with events after his studies at Lincoln University as well as his return home to the Gold Coast to serve the UGCC as its general secretary, thanks to the recommendation of Ako Adjei. He also spoke of the eventual formation of his own political party, the CPP, which enabled him to ascend to the pinnacle of his country's politics. He then issued an invitation to African Americans, then known as Negroes, to return to independent Gold Coast to assist their motherland:

> I then spoke about my hopes for the future. "We are aiming to work under democratic principles such as exist in Britain and in the United States. What we want is the right to govern ourselves, or even to misgovern ourselves." I again spoke of the needs of the Gold Coast for technicians, machinery and capital to develop its great natural resources, and explained that I was appealing to the democracies of Britain and the United States for this assistance in the first place, but that if this should not be forthcoming, I would be forced to turn elsewhere. I [also] said that there was much for the Negro people of America to do to help their ancestral country both then and in the future and that upon the attainment of independence, it was the intention of my Party to re-name the country Ghana.[33]

It is, indeed, not surprising that after Nkrumah returned home from the Lincoln University visit, several African Americans—including the Stanford University's Anthropologist Professor St. Clair-Drake and Maya Angelou, the late distinguished poet—flocked to independent Ghana. These Black men and women from the American diaspora took jobs on university campuses, and at radio and television stations. For them, they were ready to contribute to the country that Nkrumah referred to as their ancestral home.

GOLD COAST BECOMES GHANA AT INDEPENDENCE UNDER KWAME NKRUMAH'S LEADERSHIP

With independence for the Gold Coast looming, Sir Frederick Bourne, who was a British constitutional expert, was sent to the Gold Coast to serve as a constitutional advisor to assist in the creation of a new constitution for independent Gold Coast, which would become Ghana. In fact, he worked so hard that, by December 17, 1956, he handed to the governor a brand-new Gold Coast constitution. A thorny issue that reared its ugly head was whether Trans-Volta

Togoland should be annexed by the Gold Coast at independence or to be relinquished to French Togoland. To settle that question, Sir Bourne recommended a plebiscite to be supervised by the United Nations. The voters voted for Trans-Volta Togoland to become part of the Gold Coast as a Volta Region at independence.[34] Since the new constitution called for pre-independence general elections, with Dr. Kofi Abrefa (K.A.) Busia as leader of the opposition, the Gold Coast was poised to be more than ready to accomplish this task. As expected, the CPP led by Nkrumah swept the polls, and the governor asked him to form the pre-independence government.

At this point, Nkrumah named 10 cabinet ministers, with three additional cabinet-level ministers without portfolio. The ministers and the three appointees without designated positions were the following:[35]

Table 4.1 Nkrumah's Earliest Indigenous Cabinet Appointees[36]

Name	Cabinet Designation
Honorable Minister Ako Adjei	Interior Ministry
Honorable Minister Kojo Botsio	Trade and Labor Ministry
Honorable Minister K.A. Gbedemah	Finance Ministry
Honorable Minister A. Casely-Hayford	Communications Ministry
Honorable Minister A.E. Inkumsah	Housing Ministry
Honorable Minister B. Yeboah-Afari	Agriculture Ministry
Honorable Minister (Rev) J.B. Erzuah	Education Ministry
Honorable Minister N.A. Welbeck	Works Ministry
Honorable Minister J.H. Allasani	Health Ministry
Honorable Minister Aaron E Ofori-Atta	Local Government Ministry
Honorable L.R. Abavana	Minister without Portfolio
Honorable Krobo Edusei	Minister without Portfolio
Honorable Kofi Baako	Ministerial Secretary and Government Chief Whip

With these appointments, Nkrumah became anxious to know the actual day for the handover of the reins of power to him and the CPP. To allay his fears, the governor extended an invitation to Nkrumah to visit his office on September 17, 1956. In that meeting, prime minister Nkrumah was informed that Her Majesty's Government in the United Kingdom had named the date as March 6, 1957. The March 6 date was in commemoration of the Colonial Bond of March 6, 1844. Nkrumah's happiness was beyond control as he told the Gold Coast press in a brief statement after emerging from the Governor's office: "On the one hundredth and thirteenth anniversary of the [British] Bond of 1844, which led to British political domination of the Gold Coast, our country will be free."³⁷

Representing Queen Elizabeth II to present the instruments of independence, on March 6, 1957, to Prime Minister Kwame Nkrumah was the Duchess of Kent. Earlier that day, Governor Sir Charles Arden-Clarke was sworn in as the governor-general of the new Ghana while Nkrumah, too, was sworn in as the first elected prime minister, thus becoming the newest member of the British Commonwealth of Nations. It was at the event that Nkrumah, as a Pan-Africanist, said loudly to the excited crowd that Ghana's independence would be meaningless unless it was linked up with the total liberation of Africa. As Nkrumah uttered these words loudly, the crowd cheered and burst into the song, "There is Victory for Us. . . ." And an emotional Kwame Nkrumah wiped tears from his eyes with a white handkerchief telling the crowd, "Ghana, our beloved country, is free or ever. Freedom!"³⁸

POST-INDEPENDENT GHANA'S SOCIALIST DEVELOPMENTAL APPROACH

Kwame Nkrumah hailed the fact that the 5th Pan-Africanist Congress of 1945, held in Manchester, United Kingdom, rejected both capitalist and reformist solutions to the African colonial problems. As he wrote about that conference in 1957, "instead the Congress unanimously endorsed the doctrine of African socialism based upon the tactics of positive action without violence."³⁹ Indeed, Nkrumah had already implemented the positive action aspect of the declaration of the Congress, for which he and the late Kenyan president Jomo Kenyatta were the Joint Secretaries. Any careful observer, who watched Nkrumah's euphoric discussion of socialism in his published 1957 memoirs would have been able to predict his developmental path as the leader of Ghana.

However, as prime minister, with a British governor-general, he appointed cabinet members with mixed ideological backgrounds, including mainstream capitalists. Observers were of the feeling that he did so to make sure that his new and fragile government was not derailed by powerful capitalist nations. His biographer Mrs. June Milne, a British historian, made it clear that Nkrumah pursued a socialist path of development by phasing out the private sector of the economy through the expansion of the public sector rather than attempt an all-out program of nationalization. She explained the rationale in the following words:

> Immediate nationalization would have been synonymous with a declaration of war on imperialism, and this would have brought an economic blockade by the West. [Therefore] many important development projects, chief among them the Volta River Dam, would have had to be shelved. In addition, while the politicization of

the Ghanaian people was proceeding, the forces of feudalism and conservativism in Ghana were still strong. [Yet] Ghana was venturing along an uncharted road in that no other newly independent African country, with similar economic conditions, had attempted such far-reaching socialist objectives. There was, therefore, no experience on which to draw. Ghana was, in this respect, a pacesetter.[40]

Apart from Nkrumah's biographer pointing out his socialist path to development, he had himself not hidden that fact, including volunteering the information that he was an avowed socialist, eve with Marxist ideological interests. In fact, he further pointed out loudly that—not until there is an All-African union government pursuing socialist policies, and planning the economic development of Africa as a whole—the standard of living of the African masses would remain low, and that they would also "continue to suffer from neo-colonialist exploitation and the oppression of the indigenous bourgeoise."[41] Interestingly, although Nkrumah was known to have espoused socialist policies as Ghana's president, yet the need for developmental assistance did force him to seek external cooperative assistance in new projects, including Ghana's hydroelectric project, which was built on the Volta River to supply electricity to the country and its neighboring nations of Togo, Upper Volta (now Burkina Faso), and Ivory Coast. Both International Bank for Reconstruction and Development and the U.S.-based Kaiser Engineering Company invested in that project.[42]

Writing about the project in the *Financial Times* of London, correspondent Mike Faber was a lot more interested in the financial aspects. Therefore, he endeavored to inform his readers about the financial institutions involved in sponsoring the project. He, *inter alia*, wrote:

> The arrangements agreed in 1962 between President Kwame Nkrumah, Mr. Edgar Kaiser [of Kaiser Engineers Company of USA], President John F. Kennedy, the World Bank, the U.S. Exim Bank, the British Government and others led to the construction of the Volta River dam and Akosombo power station, the formation of the most extensive man-made lake in the world and the construction of Africa's largest aluminum smelter.[43]

The Essence of Kwame Nkrumah's 1961 Volta River Project in Ghana

President Kwame Nkrumah had to sell positively to the people of Ghana, through the Parliament, the need for what critics saw as the very expensive Volta River Project. Therefore, in an address to the Ghana Parliament on Tuesday, February 21, 1961, when Ghana's republican experiment was less than a year old, President Nkrumah, among other details, said:

Newer nations, such as ours, which are determined by every possible means to catch up in industrial strength, must have electricity in abundance before they can expect any large-scale industrial advance. That, basically, is the justification for the Volta River Project.[44]

Most certainly, the Volta River Project, as proposed to the Ghana Parliament, was supported overwhelmingly by Nkrumah's CPP parliamentary majority for the search to begin in earnest for Ghana, under Nkrumah's leadership, to seek international financial assistance. Interestingly, the project had a history of its own, as it dates back to 1952, when Nkrumah informed the British Government of his interest in such a venture. Submitting to the desire of the prime minister, the British Government supported the proposed project and, as it was expected, a White Paper was published by the British leaders, which suggested the need for a preparatory commission to visit every aspect of the project, including its funding prospects; it suggested the examination by such a commission to be in depth.[45]

Although Nkrumah's mind was preoccupied by his quest for Ghana independence by 1957, he also made unsuccessful efforts for funding for the Volta River Project. He then shelved the idea temporarily until Ghana attained its independence on March 6, 1957. Following the handover, Nkrumah decided to approach American leaders for assistance. During his July 1958 visit to America, he was supposed to have "talked endlessly with President [Dwight] Eisenhower."[46] Apart from the American government agreeing to share the cost for a re-appraisal of the project with the Nkrumah government, names of American companies capable of building such a venture as the Volta River Project were made available to President Nkrumah. Among them was the Henry J. Kaiser Company, which proactively went ahead to send to "Nkrumah suggestions which would reduce the capital costs of the scheme to a minimum."[47]

Although Nkrumah was impressed with the suggestions and estimates made by the Kaiser Engineering Company, he still wanted to see how best the massive amount of electricity from the Volta River Project could largely be consumed inside Ghana. That was why the Nkrumah government suggested the setting up of the Ghana aluminum smelter company, especially since Ghana produces the raw aluminum ore, a proposal that was accepted by the Kaiser side. Also, with Kaiser's interest in the project, the new Democratic Party government of President John F. Kennedy, who was later assassinated in 1963, agreed to provide the needed loans for the project, and that was in April 1961, shortly after Kennedy's inauguration.[48] Biographer Bankole Timothy pointed out that Nkrumah was pleased and ready to sign an agreement with the American company. He wrote:

> This pleased Kwame Nkrumah and, without wasting time, he signed the formal agreements between his government and the Henry J. Kaiser Company

of California. These agreements were signed in Accra [Ghana] on January 22, 1962. This was a great achievement by Nkrumah, and it justified his faith in the project. So work began on the great Volta River Project until, at last, on Saturday, January 22, 1966, Nkrumah formally inaugurated hydro-electric power from the Volta.[49]

Nkrumah hailed the inauguration of the hydroelectric power from the project in the following words:

> What you see before you is the happy result of the faith and determination of our people and their friends, It is the outcome of the readiness of the United States Government, the World Bank, and financial institutions which, apart from our own contribution to the scheme, have granted loans and other forms of assistance, in this great enterprise. It is an achievement in cooperation and joint endeavor.[50]

Nkrumah, with Pan-Africanist zeal, highly believed in promoting ventures that would promote African unity, as he was also very happy that not only Ghana was to benefit from the electricity that was to be generated; he said:

> We have enough power for our immediate needs from the Volta Dam and for the aluminium smelter which is now being constructed at Tema. But, we are ready and prepared to supply power to our neighbors in Togo, Dahomey [Benin], the Ivory Coast and Upper Volta [Burkina Faso]. As far as I am concerned, this project is not for Ghana alone. Indeed, I have already offered to share our power resources with our sister African states.[51]

Apart from direct power supply to the homes of Ghanaian citizens, Nkrumah biographer Bankole Timothy pointed out how the Volta River Project also brought about other crucial benefits. For example, "the country's industries have a good supply of electricity; the dam that was created provides fresh water for fishing purposes, while new townships were created for the resettlement of displaced citizens, with new amenities, adding: These [modern] townships have provided new homes for the 80,000 people, who had to be moved away as a result of the creation of the Volta Lake."[52] Although President Nkrumah's government was overthrown in a *coup d'etat* on February 24, 1966, forcing him to live in exile in the late president Sekou Toure's Guinea until his death from cancer in April 1972, it is recognized locally and internationally that the Volta River Project that his government promoted will remain a permanent mark of honor for his name. In fact, Sir Robert Jackson was quoted by the biographer as pointing out the following: "Whatever the future may hold, history will undoubtedly give full credit to President Nkrumah for his achievement in bringing the Volta River to life."[53]

NOTES

1. Nkrumah, autobiography, op. cit., pp. 64–65.
2. Omari, op. cit., pp. 1–2.
3. Basil Davidson, 1973. *Black Star: A View of the Life and Times of Kwame Nkrumah.* New York: Praeger, p. 59.
4. Nkrumah, op. cit., p. 87.
5. Kwame Nkrumah, op cit., p. 102.
6. Ibid., p. 102.
7. Ibid., p. 107.
8. Ibid., p. 109.
9. Ibid., p. 108.
10. IIbid., p. 111.
11. Ibid., p. 114.
12. Ibid., p. 117.
13. A.B. Assensoh. 1998. *African Political Leadership.* Malabar, FL: Krieger Publishing Company, p. 93.
14. Ibid., p. 93.
15. Ibid., p. 93.
16. Ibid., p. 94.
17. Ibid., p. 94.
18. Ibid.
19. Nkrumah, Ibid., p. 137.
20. Ibid., p. 137.
21. Ibid., pp. 94–95.
22. Kofi Buenor Hadjor. 1988. *Nkrumah and Ghana: The Dilemma of a Postcolonial Power.* London, UK: Kegan Paul, p. 58.
23. Assensoh, 1998, op. cit., p. 95.
24. Hadjor, op. cit., p. 142.
25. Ibid., p. 144.
26. Ibid., p. 158.
27. Ibid., p. 160.
28. Ibid., p. 158.
29. Ibid., p. 160.
30. Ibid., p. 160.
31. Ibid., p. 160.
32. A.B. Assensoh. 1978. *Kwame Nkrumah: Six Years in Exile, 1966–1972.* Ilfracombe, Devon, UK: Arthur Stockwell Ltd. (Publisher); Nkrumah, op. cit., 164.
33. Nkrumah, Ibid., p. 164.
34. Assensoh, 1998, op. cit., p. 98.
35. Ibid., p. 98.
36. Kwame Nkrumah, Autobiography, 1972; p. 212.
37. Ibid., p. 99; Nkrumah, p. 281.
38. Assensoh, 1998, p. 99.
39. Nkrumah, op. cit., pp. 52–53.

40. June Milne. 1974. *Kwame Nkrumah: Panaf Great Lives Series*. London: Panaf Boks (Publishers), pp. 109–110. Assensoh, 1998, op. cit., p. 99.
41. Ibid., pp. 99–100.
42. Assensoh, 1998, op. cit., pp. 100–101.
43. Mike Faber, "How Nkrumah's Dream Became a Commercial Reality," *Financial Times of London* (July 18, 1984), p. 14; Assensoh, 1998, op. cit., p. 101.
44. Bankole Timothy, op. cit., p. 41.
45. Ibid., p. 41.
46. Ibid., pp. 41–42.
47. Ibid., p. 42.
48. Ibid., p. 42.
49. Ibid., pp. 42–43.
50. Ibid., p. 43.
51. Ibid., pp. 43–45.
52. Ibid., p. 45.
53. Ibid., p. 45.

Chapter 5

Ghana

Kwame Nkrumah's Political Kingdom, 1960–1966

GHANA ATTAINS REPUBLICAN STATUS, 1960–1966

Since Ghana's opposition political leader Dr. K.A. Busia had left the country to live in Europe in a virtually self-imposed exile, mostly to teach at University of Oxford, he was succeeded by Dr. J.B. Danquah, an illustrious lawyer, who had been trained at the University of London. Dr. Danquah was also one of the UGCC leaders, who invited Nkrumah to serve their Convention as its secretary-general. He was the contestant in the general elections of June 1960 against Nkrumah as the CPP candidate for the position of Ghana's first president under the Republican constitution.

After Nkrumah and his CPP won that election, as pointed out earlier, he declared Ghana a republican nation, which meant that the Queen of England ceased to be the titular Head of State. The new status gave Nkrumah more powers to rule Ghana, which included the enactment in 1962 of Ghana's pernicious Preventive Detention Act (PDA), which was first passed to detain political opponents who were suspected of plotting against Nkrumah and his government. Several prominent opposition leaders and even critical journalists were detained, including the opposition leader, Dr. J.B. Danquah, "the very person, who paid the boat fare to enable Nkrumah to return to Gold Coast [from the U.K.] to begin his nationalist struggle."[1]

While several detention centers were established to detain such political opponents of Nkrumah, without trial, the most notorious was the Nsawam Prison. Sadly, Dr. Danquah died in this prison on February 4, 1965. Possibly remembering what Dr. Danquah did for him to enable him return home, reports were that Nkrumah was remorseful about Lawyer Danquah's death in prison, hence he left Accra, the capital of Ghana, for several days in his hometown Nkroful, in the Western Region of Ghana "for meditations and prayers, ostensibly reflecting on his life, actions and political philosophy."[2] Sadly, nothing happened as a consequence after Dr. Danquah's death, but a year later, Nkrumah was overthrown in a military-cum-police coup d'etat in February 1966.

With Ghana as a republic, Nkrumah saw the need to experiment with several of his political ideas. For example, as noted widely, Nkrumah's foreign policy was detested by his political opponents, who felt that, with his long-standing Pan-Africanist interest, Nkrumah, indeed, did more for continental politics than local Ghanaian issues.[3] In fact, Ghana's long-serving foreign minister Obed Asamoah (1936–), under the leadership of the late President Jerry John Rawlings (1947–2020)—who ruled Ghana from 1981 to 2001—did place in proper perspective some of the actions of Nkrumah in the following words:

> One of the primary pre-occupations of Nkrumah's [CPP] government was the need to make political independence meaningful by achieving the economic emancipation of Ghana and Africa, always with Africa as a companion issue.[4]

Dr. Asamoah went on to confirm that Nkrumah, at that point, was trying to fulfill his 1957 assertion that the independence of Ghana would only be meaningful if it was linked with the total liberation of the African continent. The former foreign minister in fact spoke in glowing terms the foreign policy pursued by the Nkrumah regime.[5] That, indeed, also confirmed Nkrumah's deep sense of Pan-Africanism, which has been redefined and, in this book, discussed as a chapter.

NKRUMAH'S POLICY TOWARD EDUCATION AS GHANA'S PRESIDENT

Nkrumah, as the leader of Ghana, was of the opinion that his country would benefit tremendously from the extent of the awareness of the citizenry. Therefore, he decided to invest heavily in education. Toward that end, Nkrumah made sure that the local educational institutions, prominent among them the then University College of Ghana (now University of Ghana) saw a major transformation. Toward that end, Nkrumah agreed to visit the campus of the university on October 25, 1963, to inaugurate the revamped Institute of African Studies, which was first established in 1961. The main purpose of the Institute was to promote the advancement of new knowledge about Africa, its people and culture.[6]

To ensure that the revamped Institute had a new focus, Nkrumah pointed out how African Studies, as a discipline, had been established by various universities and colleges as centers of learning, which had "been influenced by concepts of the old style colonial studies and, still to some extent, remain under the shadow of colonial ideologies and mentality."[7] In furtherance of African Studies, Nkrumah promoted the establishment of the "Encyclopedia Africana" with Dr. W.E.B. DuBois, a foremost U.S.-born Pan-Africanist, as its first Director. His foremost duties included making sure that the new encyclopedia, which was to be a strong component of African Studies, would play the role of interpreting and enhancing African history from the Pan-African perspective. Shortly after the establishment of the encyclopedia, Dr. DuBois, who had already laid the foundation for the project, fell ill and in 1963, he died and was given a befitting state funeral by the Nkrumah regime. It is reported by several sources that, upon visiting Dr. DuBois open casket, Nkrumah knelt and kissed on his forehead. Interestingly, it was on the same day of Dr. DuBois's death—August 28, 1963—that the late Reverend Dr. Martin Luther King, Jr. (1929–1968), "led his march on Washington, DC., to pressure the John F. Kennedy administration for jobs and better conditions of life for his fellow black people."[8]

While Nkrumah's focus on education in Ghana in 1960–1964 was to have a Pan-Africanist and transformative content, his political opponent, the late Dr. Busia, in self-imposed exile as sociology professor at the University of Oxford, published the book *Purposeful Education for Africa* (1964), with a foreword written by Rev. Dr. Emory Ross (1887–1973), an Indiana-born African missionary. In the introductory foreword, Dr. Ross praised Dr. Busia for writing "cogently and perceptively and, at the same time, briefly and simply about a philosophy of education for the huge, diverse complex called Africa."[9]

Dr. Ross held the highest opinion of the 1964 book as well as other contributions the former prime minister of Ghana had made to education in Africa. He added:

> This present contribution by Dr. Busia, coupled with many others he and colleagues of diverse backgrounds and experiences are making, should greatly help Africans and people of goodwill everywhere as they educate themselves and their children to use the constantly widening powers our Maker opens to us all.[10]

Although Dr. Busia was considered a conservative politician,[11] he still wrote in his 1964 book about education as a perceptive African. His own lamentation was that, as he went through college and subsequently university, he felt increasingly that the education he received mostly from European missionaries did teach him more and more about Europe, and less and less about his own African society. The Oxford-educated sociology professor went on to point out that his book tried to spell out the ends of education for Africans, and that, from his research, he realized that "Africa was in search of a social philosophy of education. Everywhere, education was expected to help fulfill national aspirations and goals."[12]

However, differing from Nkrumah's full-blown Pan-Africanist education for people of Ghana, for example, Busia felt that the educated African was taught how to cope with his environment, how to farm, hunt, or fish, or prepare food, or build a house, or run a home, similar to what America-born Booker T. Washington taught his Tuskegee Institute (now university) students. Dr. Busia harped on traditional education in this guise, whereby in African communities, the older generation passed on to the young the knowledge, the skills, the mode of behavior, and the beliefs they should have for playing their social roles in adult life; he added: "The methods were informal, the young [African] learnt by participating in activities alongside their elders. They learnt by listening, by watching, by doing. In many practical ways, they learnt how to live as members of their community."[13]

The Ghana-born sociologist (Dr. Busia) recommended traditional education to be of value and import, as he felt that education helped to inculcate a religious attitude to life: reverence toward nature and the unknown universe, adding:

> Traditional education taught a world-view based on polytheistic religions which conceived a world of many gods and spirits. The people's manifested through their religious rites, a strong sense of dependence on the Supreme Being on deities and spirits, on the departed ancestors, and on local resources: earth, rivers, food.[14]

As far as Dr. Busia was concerned, traditional education, which he preferred to what Nkrumah was preaching in classrooms of socialist Ghana, sought to produce men and women who were not self-centered, thereby pointing out:

> Though traditional Africa had many cultures, they all appear to have emphasized as a *summum bonum* [of highest good], a social sensitivity, which made one lose one's self in the group, the kinsfolk[s] were, and lived as members of one another. It was the goal of [traditional education] to inculcate this sense of belonging, which was the highest value of the cultural system. The young were educated in and for the community's way of life.[15]

In the end, Dr. Busia—when compared to Nkrumah's strident criticism of colonialism—pointed out that everywhere in Africa, in the end, there was evidence of colonialism, under which "the old world of Africa has been changed, by the invasion of European science and technology, and new ideas an institution, such as schooling. The school has been one of the factors of social change in Africa."[16]

One area that the late Dr. Busia and the late deposed President Nkrumah seemed to have a common ground was in the discussion of European colonialism, especially with reference to Portugal and Spain. He lamented:

Spain, like Portugal, has premised her policy on what appears to be an indefinite perpetuation of colonialism. The policy being pursued in Spanish Guinea discourages the use of local vernaculars, and [it] pays scant regard to African traditions. The schools are vehicles for assimilating the African population into Spanish culture and the Catholic religion; but at the pace Spain has moved, it will take centuries for the mass of the African population to qualify for political and cultural assimilation.[17]

As Ghana's prime minister, between 1969 and 1972, Dr. Busia promoted the policy of having dialogue with apartheid South Africa, which was opposed by very radical Ghanaian scholars and newspaper editors. Interestingly, however, Dr. Busia in his 1964 book did offer an interesting discussion of educational aspects of what later led to the establishment of apartheid system in South Africa. He quotes South African parliamentary documents, including the *Hansard* and debates of September 14–18, 1953, as the so-called Bantu Education Act of 1953 to "prepare the natives more effectively for their future occupations."[18]

Conversely, Dr. Busia discussed as a separate entity the implementation of the apartheid policy by the separate University Education Bill in the parliament of South Africa in March 1957, the very month in which Ghana attained its independence from the British monarchy led by Queen Elizabeth II. He noted that White South African politicians, led by the apartheid education minister, did defend the implementation of measures creating apartheid to ensure separate development but not just racial apartheid. Impressively, however, Dr. Busia pointed out in his book:

> The fact must be faced that the policy is designed not for equal, though separate development of the races, but for the assurance of permanent white domination. It has been justified on the ground that that it promotes the cultural development of the non-white races in accordance with their own traditions within a Bantu social framework. It is a philosophy of education based on the "inherent aptitudes of native races," and on a fallacious doctrine of cultural hegemony. Africans have no inborn social or cultural traits that cannot be modified by learning. Cultures do not permanently divide races. They are learnt; education can bridge cultural gulfs.[19]

Very surprisingly, in 1964, Dr. Busia sounded as if he and then-president Nkrumah had a common ground in dealing with colonialism and White supremacy issues in the colonies. The Oxford don spelled out the fact that various policies of the then-prevailing colonialists—referred to by him as White rulers—left the new nations of Africa legacies of educational philosophies premised in varying degrees on European societies and on their racial or cultural superiority or both; he added:

These are philosophies which the new nations of Africa reject. The challenge facing them is that of preparing their nationals for the duties and responsibilities of citizenship in modern self-governing States [Nations], within the interdependent community of nations. They have to develop and implement educational policies in consonance with their new status and new aspirations, and in the context of the rapid social changes of Africa, which have the pace and dimensions of a revolution.[20]

Indeed, one was expecting a robust pro-Africanist—if not outright Pan-Africanist—policies to be pursued by Dr. Busia's Progress Party (PP) government upon winning the 1969 Ghana general elections against its arch-opponent, the National Alliance of Liberals (N.A.L.) led by former finance minister under Nkrumah, Mr. K.A. Gbedemah. Sadly, however, Prime Minister Busia, instead, started to promote his so-called "Dialogue with South Africa" variation. In retrospect, several commentators and observers of Dr. Busia wondered why he was deviating from the realistic tone that he discussed in his 1964 monograph, *Purposeful Education for Africa*. It was, therefore, not surprising that a teeming number of Ghanaian college and university students and commentators, including Cameron Duodu, the editor of the government-owned *Daily Graphic newspaper*, loudly opposed the pro-South Africa policy of Dr. Busia's P.P. government. Editor Duodu was removed as editor in 1970 for his detestation of the Busia government's "apartheid dialogue" policy. Returning to journalism as a freelancer, Mr. Duodu moved to London, from where he served several London-based publications, including *The Observer and New African Magazine*.[21]

THE LITERARY LEGACY OF NKRUMAH

Nkrumah saw the need to make sure that his ideas were consummated into publishable book manuscripts, hence he had several books published as President of Ghana, some of which marked him as an enemy of certain Western nations. For example, in 1960, barely three years after Ghana's independence, he published an old manuscript as the book, *Toward Colonial Freedom*. It was followed in 1963 by *Africa Must Unite*, in which the Ghanaian leader publicly reiterated his staunch belief in Africa's unification. Therefore, it was not surprising that in the same year, the Organization of African Unity was founded in Addis Ababa, capital of Ethiopia, with Diallo Telli, Guinea's former Ambassador to the United Nations as its first secretary-general.[22]

Earlier, he had published *I speak of Freedom*, in which he championed the need for freedom for all colonialized African nations. Then, after the Congo political crisis, in which his close political ally, Congolese prime minister Patrice Lumumba, was assassinated, he wrote *Challenge of the Congo*; in the book, Nkrumah discussed the conspiracies of various major United Nations countries of the West that connived to get rid of Lumumba. He also added how the Swedish head of the United Nations, secretary-general Dag Hammarskjold (1905–1961) died in a plane crash near present-day Zambia on his way from the then Congo (now DRC). A book, written and published by Nkrumah, which created a major enmity for him among Western nations was *Neo-Colonialism: The Last Stage of Imperialism.* According to several observers, it was this 1965 book which prompted the U.S. government of late president Lyndon B. Johnson to instigate Nkrumah's overthrow a year later. In the book, he reportedly criticized Western capitalism and imperialism, as he noted that it was the last stage of both. A subsequent action taken by the Johnson administration in America was about earmarked aid for Ghana:

> In 1965, for example, Ghana was slated to receive $35 million in American foreign aid, but it was promptly cancelled. The book was [seen as] as strident attack on capitalism, multinational operations in the Third World, particularly Africa, and the operations of the Central intelligence Agency (CIA) of America. To add insult to injury, Nkrumah and his supporters made sure that an American edition of such an anti-American book was published by International Publishers of New York.[23]

Newspapers and News Media: Instruments for Enlightenment

In *Africa: An Encyclopedia of Culture and Society* (2015), Xavier University of Louisiana–based Endowed Professor Steve J. Salm has confirmed that Ghana, indeed, has had a long history of newspaper publication, as part of the materials that citizens in places like Africa read for enlightenment. Salm went on to confirm how the old capital of Cape Coast, before 1877, happened to be where newspapers flourished. He went on to chronicle impressively that, by 1960, the year that Ghana declared itself a republic, "there were 14 publications sponsored by the government in various languages . . . Government control meant one-sided news for the most part."[24]

Salm has also shown that the era of non-governmental publications in Ghana had also seen a proliferation of magazines and journals about Ghanaian political, economic, and cultural life. Their ownership varied, as churches and private entities did own some of them. Similar to the issue of newspapers, the Ghana government mostly controlled broadcasting through the issuance of licenses. However, in 1996, the Ghanaian government relaxed control of television operations by the control of the electronic media was a way for the government in power to use the medium for self-control purposes. Such private TV stations as TV 3 and Metro TV have been licensed to operate, but those who can afford it subscribe to South Africa's MNET, Channel

O, and various African sports networks, including those providing satellite TV access. Because news shows are supposed to be popular, it is also a fact that the CNN (USA) and the British Broadcasting Company (BBC) in addition provide more news, especially in the evening to broaden the perspectives of audiences on world affairs.[25]

Thanks to many years of high-quality Ghanaian TV productions, Salm confirmed that humor has had a greater impact, as it uses local images. However, there is also a fact about Ghanaian productions: "Ghanaian productions can attract a large audience share. In the meantime, Ghanaian radio and television will continue to play an important role in entertainment, education and development."[26]

NOTES

1. Assensoh, 1998, op. cit., p. 106.
2. Ibid., p. 106.
3. Ibid., p. 106.
4. Ibid., p. 106.
5. Ibid., p. 106.
6. Ibid., p. 103.
7. Ibid., p. 104
8. Ibid., p. 106.
9. K.A. Busia. 1964. *Purposeful Education for Africa*. The Hague, The Netherlands: Mouton & Co, p. 5.
10. Ibid., p. 6.
11. Ibid., p. 7.
12. Ibid., p. 9.
13. Ibid., p. 13.
14. Ibid., p. 15.
15. Ibid., p. 17.
16. Ibid., p. 19.
17. Ibid., p. 25.
18. Ibid., p. 27.
19. Ibid., pp. 27–28.
20. Ibid., p. 28.
21. Razak El-Alawa. 2017. *Graphic Online*, "Opinion: Time With Cameron Duodu" (September 9).
22. Assensoh, 1998, op. cit., p.p. 74-75.
23. Ibid., pp. 107–108.
24. Toyin Falola and Daniel Jean-Jacques. 2016. *Nkrumah*. Santa Barbara, CA: ABC-Clio., p. 550.
25. Ibid., pp. 550–551.
26. Ibid., p. 551.

Epilogue

The 1966 Coup, Exile, Death, and Cultural Legacy of Kwame Nkrumah

Before anybody is accused of having been implicated in the anti-Nkrumah coup of February 1966, deeper thought should be given to the involvement of the late general Akwasi Amankwa (AA) Afrifa as narrated in his own book *The Ghana Coup*. His plans to stage a coup d'etat against Nkrumah date back to 1962, during the Congo crisis involving then-president Kwame Nkrumah's own friend, the late prime minister Patrice Lumumba; he spells that intent clearly in the November 1966 book.[1]

Many commentators and observers on Ghana's political history have given the erroneous impression that the overthrow of the almost six-year-old Republican administration of the late president Nkrumah, executed by the combined forces of the Ghana Armed Forces and the Police Service, simply took place suddenly in the early hours of February 24, 1966. Yet, the late general Afrifa, one of the architects of the coup d'etat, did later disclose in public and private statements—including in his fall 1966 memoir *The Ghana Coup*—that, as far back as in 1962, he had thought about overthrowing the Convention People's Party regime of Nkrumah. That, indeed, was when he returned to Ghana from the then former Belgian Congo, where Nkrumah's friend, Patrice Lumumba (1925–1961) had been assassinated as the prime minister at the instigation and active plot of pro-Belgian Congolese military leaders.[2]

In the above-quoted statement, co-author A.B. Assensoh wrote in his 1978 monograph, *Kwame Nkrumah: Six Years in Exile, 1966–1972*, that Ghanaian military leaders had plans, as far back as 1962, to unseat Nkrumah as Ghana's president for one reason or the other. In the instance of the late General Afrifa, he confirmed his intentions in his own words:

On arrival at the Accra airport [now named after the 1966 coup leader as Kotoka International Airport], from the Congo (now DRC) in 1962, I was to lead the men to Tamale, our destination. I paused for a moment and reflected. Should I throw this troop of three hundred men into flag Staff House and stop the rot from continuing? Should I not by military action stop Kwame Nkrumah from leading this country towards communism? Should the destruction of individual liberty and the imposition of economic hardship not be ended through a quick and decisive military action? I must confess here that I did not, at that time, really understand communism in detail and its implications. But I knew that whatever it was, it took away freedom and denied the very fundamental liberties, which it brought to the people. In the quick moment of decision, I was prepared to act. But I did not have the courage to do this, for two reasons. My ammunition supply was limited, and my commanding officer was a way in the Congo and did not know what I was contemplating. I knew that if the operation failed, he might be executed for a plot, in which he had no hand. I was only a captain, but to me this was immaterial.³

As he pointed out in the aforementioned quotation, Afrifa's captain rank, at the time, did not matter to him at all, as he pointed out himself in his book, indeed just as it happened in Liberia with a master-sergeant seizing power in a successful coup in April 1980; therefore, the rank was immaterial, as Afrifa further commented: "A corporal with the necessary courage and belief and love for his country can topple corrupt leaders and lead a coup in a just cause."⁴ Afrifa was deeply troubled as he also felt unhappy that, with his military training, he should have been able to act decisively at the time (in 1962). At the time, he still felt that only a military action should be resorted to if one was to succeed in removing a dictator from power in an African country, in fact as he further wrote:

I always feel bitter, every time it occurs to me, that with the vastness of the problems facing Ghana, military coup was the only course to rescue our people from tyranny and alien ideologies. A coup in itself is not a good thing; but it is one of the most effective methods of restoring the constitutional rights of the people when they have been deprived of the constitutional means for changing a corrupt and tyrannical government.⁵

Afrifa was unable to put into action his interest in staging a coup d'etat between 1962 and 1964. However, he disclosed further that in 1964, two years before the actual coup took place, he returned to the coup theme. In fact, the way he approached it seemed so reckless that he could have suffered repercussions. For example, as he also disclosed in his 1966 published memoir, he had gone on an assignment to report on military exercises of the

1st Battalion of Ghana's Armed Forces at Elmina, in the Western Region of Ghana, with one Lieutenant-Colonel Crabbe as the commander. As a Brigade Commander, Afrifa traveled there in order to be able to make his required report. He disclosed in his book:

> I went to Elmina to visit the Battalion, and there I discussed with the commanding officer my plan for a coup. I persuaded him to change his exercise into an operation. There were approximately one thousand men under his command. I assured him that if we made a quick dash for Accra in the night we could arrest Nkrumah and topple the Convention People's Party government.[6]

Apart from Afrifa detesting the foreign socialist ideology that Nkrumah was supposed to be preaching in Ghana at this time, he also had other ulterior motives. An example was the fact that he was appalled at the faded military apparel/clothes worn by the Ghanaian soldiers, effectively describing the uniforms as being tattered. This was because the Nkrumah regime lacked foreign currency to import uniform for their use. Afrifa confessed in his book that their clothes/uniforms were virtually in tatters, and that they also had no adequate ammunition, adding: "The burden of taxation [on Ghanaians] was heavy. The cost of living for the ordinary soldier [of Ghana] was high. The Army was virtually at the mercy of the politicians, who treated it with arrogance and open contempt."[7]

While Afrifa and some of his military cohorts were unhappy with the Nkrumah government by 1965, an area of Ghana that was developing fast was the focus on women. Nkrumah was being commended by observers that women were being well integrated in governmental affairs as cabinet-level positions were given to them as well. In fact, Professor Florence Abena Dolphyne of the University of Ghana had some laudable comments on this issue of women in her book, *The Emancipation of Women: An African Perspective* (1991). She had, herself, studied locally and in the United Kingdom earning her doctoral (PhD) degree. She, among other details, pointed out that Ghana could boast of its female population having several well-educated folks to rub shoulders with their male counterparts.[8]

As proof of the height at which women had risen under Nkrumah, Dr. Dolphyne, a trained linguist, rose through the ranks of University of Ghana to become the pro-vice-chancellor. It was only her retirement age which stopped her from becoming the first female vice-chancellor or head of University of Ghana, at her undergraduate *alma mater*. Very impressively, she also became the chairperson of the Ghana National Council on Women and Development, one of the few such women well trained during the Nkrumah era for possible major national positions.[9]

Epilogue

THE BEGINNING OF THE END OF KWAME NKRUMAH'S CPP GOVERNMENT

By 1965, the government of Kwame Nkrumah under his CPP leadership was becoming very notorious for its detention of political opponents without trial under what was known as the Preventive Detention Act (PDA), as briefly mentioned earlier. In the book *Politics of Political Detention* (1971), Kwame Kesse-Adu, the city editor of *The Pioneer* newspaper of Kumasi, Ghana, took pains to write about his own arrest and detention without trial as a journalist; he also discussed the similar plight meted out to several other Ghanaians, who were considered opponents of the Nkrumah regime. Apart from the one-party rule espoused by the Nkrumah regime during this time, University of Ghana Professor K.A. Ninsin put it best when he discussed what was seen as the division within the ranks of the political elite in Ghana dating back to the early 1950s. At this time, it had become obvious that the Nkrumah regime did not respect the fundamental human rights of the citizenry guaranteed by the constitution in Ghana, especially as the government utilized the PDA either to detain indigenous political opponents or even to deport critical international personalities. The foreign deportees included the West Africa–based Anglican Archbishop C.J. Patterson and the Accra-based Anglican Bishop R.R. Roseveare, both of whom were declared *persona non grata* in August 1965, and never allowed to re-enter Ghana.[10]

Unfortunately, the most abused law enacted by the Nkrumah regime was the PDA, with which Nkrumah also detained Dr. J.B. Danquah, the much respected Ghanaian jurist, who used his own funds to pay the travel fare to enable the future president Nkrumah to return to the then Gold Coast from the United Kingdom to serve as the general-secretary of the U.G.C.C. at the time. On February 4, 1965, when the University of London-educated lawyer died in Nkrumah's political prison at Nsawam, the death was condemned by even non-Ghanaian political leaders, including Nigeria's first indigenous president Nnamdi Azikiwe, who also played a role in Nkrumah's decision to travel to Lincoln University in Pennsylvania for some of his academic degrees.[11]

Many observers of the political scene of Ghana felt very strongly that the death of Dr. Danquah in political prison, in 1965, spelt a doom for Nkrumah's leadership of Ghana. Although Nkrumah did not publicly make any statement after the announcement of the death, it has been recalled that he appeared remorseful. With suggestion, he left Accra, the capital, for a period of fast and prayers at Nkroful, his place of birth. However, the fact that Dr. Azikiwe of Nigeria, who condemned the death of Dr. Danquah, aged almost 70 years in unpleasant circumstances, in 1965, did not speak well of Nkrumah and his regime. The then Ghanaian president in his published 1957 memoir, titled *Ghana: Autobiography of Kwame Nkrumah*, showed his respect for Dr. Azikiwe as he wrote, among other details, that his decision to study at Lincoln University in 1935, he honed his nationalistic instincts by reading articles written in *The African Morning Post* by Dr. Azikiwe, an Igbo from Onitsha, Eastern Nigeria. Nkrumah pointedly confirmed: "I had first met him [Azikiwe] after he had addressed a meeting of the Gold Coast Teachers' Association some years earlier in Accra, I had been greatly impressed by him and had been more determined than ever [at the time] to go to America."[12]

Dr. Azikiwe, the Nigerian nationalist, who was practicing journalism in the then Gold Coast, seemed to be a genuinely nice person for varied reasons, especially in condemning the death of Dr. Danquah in Nkrumah's political prison. For example, Nkrumah himself confirmed his respect for him on the eve of his departure for America in search of the proverbial golden fleece, future Ghanaian president, *inter alia*, wrote as far back as in 1935:

> I boarded the motor vessel, *Apapa*, at Takoradi and was shown into a third-class cabin. In these strange surroundings, I felt desperately alone and sat on my bunk [bed] close to tears. But as providence would have it, looking suddenly on the bed, I saw a telegram. When I opened the envelope, I found it was from Nnamdi Azikiwe and read: "Goodbye. Remember to trust in God and in yourself." These few words, so well timed, at once cheered me. I began to count my blessings and remind myself that this, after all, was the beginning of all that I had planned and saved for.[13]

That the same Dr. Azikiwe, who had such a humane touch toward the young Nkrumah in 1935, to turn around to be one of several African nationalists and political leaders to criticize Nkrumah for allowing his political opponent (Dr. Danquah) to languish and die in his political prison was indeed a pointer to Nkrumah's political demise. That, indeed, was why the end of Nkrumah was predicted, and it would come very fast, almost exactly a year after the death of Dr. Danquah in February 1965 in his political prison. Sadly, for Nkrumah's supporters, Dr. Danquah's death was a dark blot on his earned fame. For example, when former U.S. distinguished diplomat and Ambassador Thomas Patrick Melady was planning to write the book *Profiles of African Leaders* (1961), he listed several African leaders, whom he had previously met, including Ethiopia's Emperor Haile Selassie, Liberia's W.V.S. Tubman, Senegal's Leopold Sedar Senghor, and Ghana's Kwame Nkrumah, stating that he was highly impressed with them. He added:

> I was so enthusiastic about the quality of the African leaders that I had just met on the African trip that I decided to write a book. They were men with human weaknesses, but this group of leaders at the historical period of the 1960s in Africa was extraordinary. I circulated my plan for a book on African leaders.

Several publishers responded with interest, and the Macmillan Company offered me a contract.[14]

The co-authoring couple, the Meladys, were correct about human weaknesses that one could find among African leaders like Nkrumah, whose political benefactor Dr. Danquah died in his political prison without trial and with no specific prison term. All of such undemocratic actions, on the part of the Nkrumah regime, culminated in the ills that led to the overthrow of the Republican regime on the morning of February 24, 1966, while Nkrumah was in China as part of his planned trip to North Vietnam to mediate in the war with America. Led by Ghana Army's Second Infantry Brigade Commander (the then Colonel Emmanuel K. Kotoka), the coup leaders established the National Liberation Council (NLC), which promptly announced that the coup was "to save Ghana from Nkrumah's rampant economic mismanagement." On that day, imprisoned political opponents of the overthrown regime were freed and allowed to go home.[15]

Post-Nkrumah Ghana, 1966–1969: "What Went Wrong"—Commissions of Enquiry

In order to see South Africa reconcile and atone for its past atrocities under apartheid brutalities, the then-president Nelson Mandela did usher in what has since become very famous as a Reconciliation Commission. It heard hearings for former police, military officers, political and liberation movement leaders to confess, atone for, and seek forgiveness for past wrongs, which included murderous brutalities. Interestingly, when the anti-Kwame Nkrumah coup d'etat took place in Ghana on February 24, 1966, commissions to probe past wrongs were established, the most famous of which was the Justice Apaloo Assets Commission, headed by Justice Frederick K. Apaloo (1921–2000) who probed into the assets and alleged graft of the deposed president. Among issues that were carefully scrutinized were last *wills* and testaments of Nkrumah, in which he had allotted several sums of money and properties to his Egyptian wife, his aged mother, his Convention People's Party (CPP), and others.[16]

Sadly, at such commissions of enquiry, and there were several, former sycophantic associates of Nkrumah denounced him. The people of Ghana were shocked that even top cabinet members, like Ghana's former defense minister Kofi Baako and top Economic Adviser E. Ayeh-Kumi, participated in criticizing and denouncing Nkrumah. Also, it was during these enquiries that it was revealed that other cabinet ministers had illegally acquired assets. Several of these former Nkrumah allies and cabinet members were made to forfeit their assets. Interestingly, however, some African leaders, at the time, did not believe the reports about Nkrumah's graft and ill-gotten assets. For example, the then Tanzanian president Julius K. Nyerere (1922–1999) refused to recognize the new military government known as the NLC. In fact, while celebrating Nkrumah's 59th birthday on September 18, 1968, in Guinea, where he was in exile, the then Zambian president Kenneth Kaunda publicly praised the Ghanaian leader, describing him as a great son of Africa.[17]

It is worth noting that Ghanaian Lawyers, who played an active part in probing Nkrumah and publishing adverse commission reports to the delight of the ruling military-*cum*-police leaders, were rewarded in variety of ways, although several of such legal experts were considered competent and deserving of their elevations. For example, the head of the Apaloo Assets Commission, Justice Apaloo was seconded to Kenya as a Chief Justice from 1993 to 1995, which was after he had also served Ghana as a Chief Justice for nine years (1977 to 1986). In spite of these happenings, the political situation in Ghana was so unstable. While Nkrumah was still in exile in nearby Guinea, two young military officers —Lieutenant S.B. Arthur and second Lieutenant Moses Yeboah – plotted and led an unsuccessful counter-coup d'etat against the NLC in April 1967. However, they succeeded in assassinating the NLC coup leader (General Emmanuel K. Kotoka and a few other military officers). Both officers were apprehended, as their counter-coup failed, and were eventually publicly executed.[18]

NLC MILITARY GOVERNMENT HANDS OVER POWER TO ELECTED CIVILIAN GOVERNMENT

It is the contention of political scientists and historians that military coups breed counter-coups. It therefore was no surprise that the April 1967 unsuccessful insurrection was staged in an attempt to replace the Kotoka administration. Perhaps, to avoid another coup attempt, it became evident that the NLC leadership would hand over power to an elected civilian regime without delay. That decision led to the preparation for civilian rule. With the help of the German Government, a Center for Civic Education was set up in Ghana with Professor K.A. Busia as its head to assist in re-educating Ghanaians on the efficacy and importance of partisan politics in national governance. Also, a new constitution was written and approved for the purpose. Multi-party elections were slated to take place in September 1969 with plans to install an elected civilian government for the start of a Second Republic, by October 1, that year.[19]

Ghana and its citizenry, at this time, became poised for a new government. Professor Busia, who returned from a self-imposed exile in Oxford and was leading the Center for Civic Education, formed the Progress Party (PP), while his main opponent, former Nkrumah finance minister Gbedemah, formed the

National Alliance of Liberals (NAL); there were other minor political parties, which did not do well in the elections that was won overwhelmingly by Professor Busia. On October 1, 1969, Busia was publicly sworn into office, and he chose to be the prime minister with executive powers. However, he would only rule for less than three years.[20]

As Prime Minister Busia and his PP regime were in power in Ghana, the deposed President Kwame Nkrumah was busy at work in Guinea, where he had been received with honors by the then-president Ahmed Sekou Toure. what irritated Busia and the 1966 anti-Nkrumah coup leaders was the fact that upon his government's overthrow, Nkrumah did not only seek political asylum in Guinea. Instead, Guinean leaders made it abundantly clear that they were indebted to Nkrumah whose government loaned U.S. $10 million to Guinea, when the French left and pulled out most installations, including even chalk boards in classrooms and withdrew French workers. It was this sense of gratitude that inspired Guinea's ruling Parti Democratique de Guinea (or the Democratic Party of Guinea, PDG) to extend an official invitation to Nkrumah and his accompanying entourage to reside in Guinea following the overthrow of that regime. Additionally, upon his arrival, on March 2, 1966, in the capital of Conakry, Sekou Toure announced at a mammoth rally that the deposed Ghanaian president was being appointed "Co-President of Guinea, [which] demonstrated the militancy of the people of Guinea and the strength of their Pan-Africanism."[21]

From Guinea, Nkrumah published several monographs, mostly critiquing the Ghanaian political scene, of which the most critical was titled *Dark Days in Ghana* (1968). In it, Nkrumah wrote unequivocally that his arrival in Guinea on March 2, 1966, was "one of the most fruitful and happiest periods of my life."[22] Also, to show that Nkrumah's co-presidency announcement was neither a ruse nor a propaganda stunt, his publishers, among other details, confirmed:

> From his arrival until August of 1971, when he [Nkrumah] was compelled to leave Conakry for medical treatment in Bucharest, [Romania], Nkrumah worked side by side with Sekou Toure, the PDG and the people of Guinea. During those years, he wrote five books, four pamphlets, and made many broadcasts to the Ghanaian people. He was in contact with African and other world leaders. He was in daily consultation with Sekou Toure and members of the Guinean Government and PDG. The African people will forever be indebted to Guinea for protecting Nkrumah and for making it possible for him to continue his work.[23]

Furthermore, the seriousness of Dr. Nkrumah about his revolutionary activities in Guinea has been confirmed by his publishers in the following words:

He and the Ghanaians with him at Villa Syli underwent courses of military training with units of the people's militia, and [he] regularly attended political meetings. On all important state occasions, Nkrumah could be seen at the side of Sekou Toure, his last appearance in public being his presence at the people's Supreme Court in January 1971 when the Guinean National Assembly met to consider the cases of the prisoners arrested during and after the invasion of 22 November 1970. Nkrumah was then a very sick man, but he insisted on being present to show his support for Sekou Toure on that very difficult occasion. It was appropriate that it was in Conakry that Nkrumah reached the height of his revolutionary stature.[24]

THE END: NKRUMAH'S DEATH IN 1972 IN BUCHAREST, ROMANIA, AND SUBSEQUENT EVENTS

Guinea's Co-President, Dr. Kwame Nkrumah, left Guinea in 1971 for Bucharest to receive medical attention for a cancerous illness. He was, in fact there, in 1972 being treated for the illness when, on January 13, of that year, the government of Prime Minister Busia was overthrown in a military coup d'etat, led by the then colonel Ignatius Kutu Acheampong of the Ghana Army. Nkrumah was very ill at the time, but he reportedly inquired if he had been invited to return to Ghana after the Acheampong coup. He was disappointed that no such invitation came from the new rulers, who instituted the National Redemption Country (NRC) and appointed an admixture of military and civilian cabinet members to replace the PP government of Prime Minister Busia who was at the time in Oxford, United Kingdom, seeking medical help for an ailment. Unfortunately for his political supporters and family, Nkrumah died at the Romanian clinic on Thursday, April 27, 1972. And, very swiftly, the Guinean government of the then-president Sekou Toure made sure that three days after his death, on April 30, 1972, his mortal remains were flown to the Guinean capital, Conakry.[25]

The late Guinean president Sekou Toure, the ruling PDG, and the people of Guinea were determined to honor in death the deposed Ghanaian leader and the Guinean co-president. Therefore, two days of national mourning—May 13–14, 1972—was declared and reported in the following words:

> Two days of national mourning was declared. Guineans of all walks of life attended, leaders of African national liberation movements, and a delegation from Ghana's new regime, the National Redemption Council (NRC) attended the funeral. It was at the funeral that Guinea-Bissau liberation movement leader Amical Cabral described Nkrumah's cancer as "cancer of betrayal."[26]

As his Panaf publishers reported, Guineans honored Nkrumah as their co-president in the following manner:

> Units of the Guinean armed forces, people's militia, workers' brigade, and women's and youth organizations marched past, the coffin bearing Nkrumah's remains was draped with the Guinean flag, was taken to the mausoleum in a park in central Conakry. There it was placed beside the tomb of Guinea's national hero, Samory Toure.[27]

Several of Nkrumah's supporters and his immediate family, including his Egyptian widow (Mrs. Fathia Nkrumah), wanted his mortal remains to be returned and buried in Ghana. Therefore, negotiations went on for that to happen. The Guinean government, as reported, agreed to release the body to the new military government in Ghana due to the personal intervention of General Yakubu Gowon, the then Nigerian military Head of State, who reportedly appealed on behalf of the late former president Nkrumah's family back in Ghana. That was why the casket containing the remains was flown to Ghana on July 7, 1972, aboard a Guinean Airline (Air Guinea) for a memorial service in the Ghanaian capital, Accra, and a subsequent temporary burial in his birthplace of Nkroful.[28]

Eventually, Nkrumah's remains were exhumed and reburied in a national mausoleum in Accra befitting the status of the leader, who achieved independence for Ghana. Ironically, however, it was also due partly to the hard work of the then NRC Roving Ambassador Joe Appiah working in concert with Nigeria's General Gowon that it became possible for Nkrumah to be buried in Ghana after all. The irony was that Ambassador Appiah, a senior Adviser to the ruling NRC military government, negotiated with Guinea for Nkrumah's remains. Lawyer Appiah was for many years Nkrumah's political associate until they had irreconcilable differences, causing Mr. Appiah, reportedly, to suffer political detention under Nkrumah's PDA. Ghanaians are grateful that it was under the leadership of the late President Rawlings that Ghana erected the mausoleum to honor the former late president Nkrumah.[29]

TAKING STOCK: EXPLANATION FOR SOME OF NKRUMAH'S ACTIONS AS LEADER OF GHANA

Ghana's late president Kwame Nkrumah has been dead since 1972, and he is now entombed in the magnificent mausoleum in Accra. Yet, at national and international conferences, Nkrumah's leadership is still debated and written about by scholars from all walks of life. Indeed, several scholars and pundits have wondered about the reasons behind some of his actions when he held political power, especially the retention of the PDA, which was put in place legislatively in 1958. The law was similar to an earlier law that was established in India to deal with the political opponents of the Asian nation in the desire to counteract terrorist activities.[30]

Nkrumah very interestingly had a fascination for Indian nationalist leader Mahatma Gandhi. In fact, when Nkrumah planned to undermine the British colonial authorities to force decolonization, he introduced what he termed as "Positive Action," which he summed up as follows:

> I described Positive Action as the adoption of all legitimate and constitutional means by which we could attack the forces of imperialism in the country [Gold Coast]. The weapons were legitimate political agitation, newspaper and educational campaigns and, as a last resort, the constitutional application of strikes, boycotts and non-cooperation based on the principle of absolute non-violence, as used by Gandhi in India.[31]

Observers of Nkrumah's politics have often pointed out that most of the tyrannical measures he adopted in postcolonial Ghana to bring about law and order were put in place through parliamentary action, never illegally. For example, when his political opponents threatened mayhem and the use of extra-judicial measures to create instability in the new Ghana, Nkrumah decided to seek parliamentary support to introduce measures that were similar to what India introduced and also promulgated by the British in Northern Ireland. However, when the C.P.P. government of Nkrumah, in July 1958, used parliamentary measures to introduce the PDA, Ghana-born Professor L. H. Ofosu-Appiah (1920–1990) publicly examined how the law — similar to what colonialist officials in India for stability — would allow Nkrumah and his government to arrest and indefinitely detain suspected terrorists and individuals, who would promote unrest and, as a result, criticized the law, adding: "that [the date] marked the end of civil and political liberties in Ghana."[32]

Although Professor Ofosu-Appiah could easily be seen as being biased ethnically against the Nkrumah government, it was also a fact that non-Ghanaian scholars and journalists considered the PDA to be pernicious and capricious. For example, Sierra Leone–born Bankole Timothy, a famous journalist and an early Nkrumah biographer—who was eventually deported from Ghana—wrote that the PDA was merely put in place "to enable Nkrumah to clamp into gaol [jail] a large number of his political opponents, including Dr. [J.B.] Danquah, Joseph [or Joe] Appiah, son-in-law of the late Sir Stafford Cripps [of United Kingdom], and Victor Owusu [a future presidential candidate]."[33]

Defenders of Nkrumah's detention and deportation measures, in the end, cited national security and stability interest for Nkrumah's actions. For example, the earliest assassination attempt on the life of the Ghanaian president on August 11, 1962, was always a case in point. On that day a young schoolgirl, by the name of Elizabeth Asantewaa, went to present a bouquet of flowers to Nkrumah at Kulungugu, a small town in Ghana's Upper East Region. Unfortunately, the hidden grenade in the bouquet of flowers went off causing the girl serious bodily harm and also to lose a leg during the presentation.[34] Also, on January 2, 1964, 23-year-old Seth Nicolas Ametwee, a Ghana policeman, tried to assassinate Nkrumah at his residence, but the bullet instead killed his security officer. On April 7, 1964, the convicted policeman [Ametwee] was sentenced to death by an Accra High Court.[35] The policeman, who had pleaded not guilty to the assassination attempt and the murder of Nkrumah's security guard, said the guard's death was accidental after the bullet missed president Nkrumah. He admitted having pointed his rifle at the president and having fired. The defendant said the former Police Commissioner Samuel Amaning, who was in detention, had allegedly persuaded him to kill President Nkrumah. He further alleged that Mr. Amaning promised him $5,600 and a trip to the United States, if he carried out the killing.[36]

The foregoing details transparently confirmed some of the reasons, which prompted the late president Nkrumah of Ghana to take extra-judicial measures—including his infamous Preventive Detention Act, PDA—to protect himself as well as the functionaries of his Convention People's Party (CPP), regime which was swiftly overthrown at dawn on Thursday, February 24, 1966 by the combined forces of the Ghana Armed Forces and the Police Service.

KWAME NKRUMAH'S POST-1966 IDEOLOGY: NKRUMAISM

While in political power as Ghana's de facto president-for-life in a one-party Republic of Ghana, Nkrumah made sure that the former Gold Coast and its citizenry were given a heavy dosage of his socialist ideology in theory and in practice. The theoretical part was imparted through educational institutions, including the Winneba-based Kwame Nkrumah Ideological Institute, where his novel Nkrumaism ideology was taught by political party (C.P.P.) leaders. The practical side, however, was spread for the consumption of the citizenry, young and old, in his five-year developmental programs, which were often infused with socialist planning that had been carefully cultivated by the British and Socialist bloc-trained economic advisers. Among them was the British Knighted St. Lucia–born Sir William Arthur Lewis (1915–1991), the 1979 Nobel Economic Science laureate. To the proponents of socialist development, it would be wrong to think that a country's liberation struggle for decolonization ends after ridding the country of colonial rule. However, for Nkrumah, "such a view was not only wrong but also extremely dangerous."[37]

Indeed, an important feature of socialist planning, which was conceived by Nkrumah as the leader of Ghana, was that the part played by the state in economic activities should be intensive. He added:

> Our planning [in Ghana] will be geared to our policy of increasing governmental participation in the nation's economic activities, and all enterprises are expected to accept this policy.... national planning must be geared to socialism. There is a great amount of confused thought on what constitutes socialist planning.[38]

Meanwhile, Nkrumah and his supporters pointed out that, in some cases, "planning" has been used as an instrument for establishing or boosting capitalism. In the light of the foregoing, as pointed out by the pro-Nkrumah editors of *Essential Features of Socialism*, the 1975 book was published to lay bare the late president's socialist thoughts:

> In the light of the foregoing, Nkrumah's teachings clearly elucidated these elements, which when taken together did constitute socialist planning. These are enumerated as follows: a mixed economy; new institutions or agencies for economic activity to be created; relations in agriculture must be recast in in order to allow a big upsurge in agricultural production; the nation itself should be the main source of development capital; a guarantee of a basic minimum standard of living for all; a steady build-up of trained manpower; industrial planning to encourage the setting up of plants; investment policy to promote local industry; and active participation of the people.[39]

Above all, Nkrumah's major principle for socialist development established unequivocally that all available foreign capital must be obtained in a way that would leave full economic control of the economy in the hands of the emergent nation. Furthermore, Nkrumah did assert that "a foreign company operating for profit in an under-developed country [should have] nothing to do with aid. Our circumstance demands that we seek capital from outside."[40] While Nkrumah's editors have used the 1975 book to advance his socialist thoughts, as espoused in his books and *The Spark* newspaper of Ghana, he himself in his published autobiography—*Ghana: The Autobiography of Kwame Nkrumah* (1972)—pointed out how, apart from all of his academic work, he endeavored to acquaint himself "with as many political organizations in the United States as I could," which included socialists and capitalists, while, as he further indicated, he also "read Hegel, Karl Marx, Engels, Lenin, and Mazzini."[41]

As his country men and women knew, deposed President Kwame Nkrumah attended American universities, and this was at a time that his ideas were evolving ideologically; one would have thought that his ideological ideas, which tended to be socialist, would have been absorbed from campus associations and activities. However, a recent discussion of ideological diversity on American campuses has underscored how that could also not have been possible. In discussing recent American graduates and their experiences with ideological diversity in *Journal of Diversity in Higher education*, Mathew R. Johnson and Jennifer Peacock, both of Central Michigan University, have pointed out how American "higher education faces mounting societal scrutiny regarding the ideological diversity it fosters, namely, in public 4-year colleges."[42]

Since Lincoln University, established in 1854 and attended by Nkrumah, was a four-year institution with courses akin to current four-year institutions, one could see why he did not suggest that his socialist ideological underpinnings emanated from his four years on that campus. Instead, both authors quoted some of the prestigious publications from campus leaders, which have shown hostility toward ideological diversity, notably the following: Bloom's 1987 book, *The Closing of the American Mind*; Bok's 1982 book, *Beyond the Ivory Tower* as well as Sacks and Thiel's 1998 book, *The Diversity Myth*. The authors added:

> Each of these books caught national attention for their attention and their criticism of higher education's hostility toward what is often coined [as] "ideological diversity"—whereby ideology is conceptualized as a comprehensive framework that comprises one's values, ideals, and attitudes about society and provides a lens to understand social and political arrangements.[43]

Very similar to what one learns from Nkrumah's discussion of his knowledge of diverse ideological awareness in his published autobiography, we also learn that ideological diversity is described as "the practice of making space for various thoughts, ideas, and perspectives, [and] that ideologies form as a result of dynamic intersection with the social world based on one's identities, thoughts, and experiences."[44]

After all, today, Dr. Nkrumah is not alive, yet his ideological underpinnings stemming from his cumulative thoughts, known as Nkrumaism, are still with us. That, indeed, is why the Ghana Young Pioneer Movement, formed to infuse education and discipline in the youth of Nkrumah's Ghana, always shouted at the top of their voices at parades when their leader was in political power: "Nkrumah never dies!" They did so because of the transformative education they attained; as Hadjor spelled out in *On Transforming Africa* (1987): "Education is a powerful instrument for instilling in people the conviction . . . that the world is there to be made."[45]

It is obvious that the education imparted to the youth of Nkrumah's Ghana sought to transform them to become Pan-Africanists in future. That, in fact, was why Hadjor added:

For education to serve its [true] purpose of the liberation of the intellect, it must be taken out of the hands of the elites. Even, with the best of intentions, a system of education cannot be developed by educators alone. The foundation of education must be built around the experience of Africa's people.[46]

In ideological terms, Ghana's late president Kwame Nkrumah went further earlier in his life to demonstrate his interest in Marxist socialism. Hence, he wrote in his autobiography that, at the 5th Pan-African Congress of 1945, most of the future African leaders attending the event became African nationalists, who revolted against colonialism, racialism, and imperialism and, in the end, adopted Marxist socialism as their philosophy. Therefore, it was not surprising that when Hadjor met Nkrumah in Guinea, after his 1966 overthrow from power, he urged him—as an African Journalist—to speak the truth about him: "You African Journalists," he shouted, "must tell the world who I actually am—a convinced Marxist socialist."[47]

THE BITTER END: NKRUMAH, A HERO OR A COMMON DICTATOR?

The late president Kwame Nkrumah of Ghana, in the end, is seen in varied ways and descriptions following his overthrow and after his death. There are enough facts and arguments to enable anyone to form an assessment of the late president. For example, the British Broadcasting Corporation (BBC) in a December 2008 survey of its African listeners concluded that Ghana's late president Kwame Nkrumah had overwhelmingly been voted by the listeners as "Man of the Millennium." However, after the military coup d'etat that removed him from power, various accounts were given of his dictatorial tendencies. Biographer Bankole Timothy, who earlier in his journalistic career had a favorable picture of Nkrumah, in 1974 gave an unflattering account of Nkrumah as part of his slim book *Kwame Nkrumah: who brought independence to Ghana*.

The Sierra Leone–born author discussed several of Nkrumah's remarkable achievements as Ghana's leader, but he reserved a section of his book to show how he became a dictator. Happily, we have shown above some of the diabolical events, which prompted some of the dictatorial actions, including the introduction of the PDA. Bankole Timothy, among varied details, wrote:

> After the success, Kwame Nkrumah began to build himself up as a sort of superman. He embarked on all sorts of schemes, which eventually led to his unpopularity and, later, his downfall. First, at a time, when Ghana needed much

money for development, he decided to build a six-meter high statue of himself with public funds, and had it erected in front of the Parliament building.⁴⁸

To Sierra Leone-born Bankole Timothy, as a non-citizen of Ghana, it was a waste of money for Nkrumah to have built and erected what was seen as a six-meter statue, which was destroyed in the aftermath of the 1966 coup that overthrew him. Fortunately, President John Jerry Rawlings, himself a former military leader-turned elected civilian president, caused a mausoleum to be built in Accra for Nkrumah's remains and that of his wife to be entombed in it; next to the mausoleum is a brass statue of the man. Apart from rehashing the story about the detention and subsequent death of opposition leader Dr. J.B. Danquah, Bankole Timothy also wrote about Dr. Danquah's successor as opposition leader (Dr. K.A. Busia):

> Dr. K.A. Busia one of the Opposition leaders, and [K.A.] Gbedemah fled the country; they were followed by some very able and senior Ghanaian civil servants. Yet the Ghana coat-of-arms bore the words: "Freedom and Justice" as the motto. But inside Ghana terror reigned supreme.⁴⁹

Sadly, Nkrumah critics, including Bankole Timothy, probably did not care to know that some of the anti-Nkrumah opposition members were alleged to be behind the lawlessness, including assassination attempts on Nkrumah's life, which sometimes either killed or maimed innocent Ghanaians. Furthermore, some of Nkrumah's political allies in his inner circle supported the PDA and other seemingly inimical legislation but later shied away from unflinching support of the policies when the political climate was unfavorable to the former president. Mr. Gbedemah, for example, was such a high-placed cabinet member—finance minister—who could not be either oblivious or innocent of the intrigues that led to the introduction of those laws.

Many readers will be either intrigued or interested in perusing the information we are quoting from Bankole Timothy and others to explain that Nkrumah did release some of his political opponents jailed under the PDA. That is contrary to the public announcement, via radio and television, that it was only after the February 24, 1966, anti-Nkrumah coup d'etat that all political prisoners were released. It was confirmed publicly that "Nkrumah released in May 1962 the first batch of political prisoners whom he had detained, but in August of the same year he detained Ako Adjei, his old colleague at Lincoln University who had later become his foreign minister. He was followed by many others."⁵⁰

When the Organization of African Unity (OAU, now known as the African Union, AU) was being formed in May 1963 in the Ethiopian capital of Addis Ababa, Nkrumah was a leading proponent. His speech there was very memorable, as he made it abundantly clear that while he was strongly in support of

African Unity, he did not care about leadership roles and where the capital of a united Africa would be cited. In a somewhat selfless manner, he and several radical African leaders instigated that Guinean ambassador to the United Nations Diallo Telli should become the first secretary-general rather than someone from their own countries. Yet, Bankole Timothy, among other details, sadly wrote:

> Instead of grappling with the grave problems facing Ghana, Nkrumah had visions of becoming the Leader of Africa and so he resurrected the idea of African unity. He wanted this to be achieved within his lifetime. He was influential in founding the Organization of African Unity (OAU) and involved himself in matters affecting other countries and the world at large. It was this outside involvement, which contributed a great deal to Nkrumah's downfall.[51]

Although Nkrumah's critics often made him seem the most unreasonable postcolonial political leader that emerged, some of his actions and speeches demonstrated differently. For example, his staunch desire for African unity which he often underscored would signify great strength for African nations. It was similar to his strong opposition to the ejection of colonialists from African territories, as he told his Lincoln University audience when getting his honorary doctoral (LL.D.) degree:

> We are aiming to work under democratic principles such as exist in Britain and in the United States. What we want is the right to govern ourselves, or even to misgovern ourselves. I again spoke of the needs of the Gold Coast for technicians, machinery and capital to develop its great natural resources and explained that I was appealing to the democracies of Britain and the United States for this assistance in the first place, but that if this should not be forthcoming, I would be forced to turn elsewhere.[52]

In discussing Ghana and Nkrumah through the lens of either a critic or an opposition element, it was often mentioned that Nkrumah, who told American audiences that his government would welcome a strong opposition to keep it on its toes, was often described as driving away his opponents into exile, with names of Professor Busia, former finance minister Gbedemah, and others mentioned repeatedly. It was also easily forgotten that Nkrumah once declared a general amnesty for his opponents in self-imposed exile. Dr. Busia, in a BBC interview, made it clear that accepting the amnesty was like signing his own death warrant. Without his hands being forced, Nkrumah made it clear in his June 1951 commencement address back at Lincoln University that he and his government "are aiming to work under democratic principles such as exist in Britain and the United States."[53] Maybe, what was necessary at the time was for Ghana's opposition leaders to promise to cooperate with President Nkrumah, instead of some of them striving as hard as possible to ensure his downfall, including instigating assassination attempts on Nkrumah's life.

Therefore, both the foreign and opposition journalists did forget that several attempts had been made on the life of Nkrumah, while he was president of the country. Therefore, it is surprising that they made it seem unreasonable for the Ghanaian leader to have tight security. Predicting the fall of Nkrumah, Bankole Timothy, among other details, wrote: "From 1962 onwards, Kwame Nkrumah surrounded himself with tight security, for he was aware of his unpopularity." According to these journalists, Nkrumah—since he became the president of Ghana—on July 1, 1960—had become a dictator because of his actions.[54]

Cultural Legacy Remaining Intact

> One abiding effect of the leadership of [Kwame] Nkrumah is that the peoples of Africa now have a consciousness of their cultural identity and possess a definite pride of culture. Africans are also aware of the need, in fact of the necessity, to discover their cultural heritage and develop it.[55]

The foregoing words were spelled out by University of Ghana's Institute of African Studies' Senior Research Fellow George P. Hagan in "Nkrumah's Cultural Policy," which was published in the late Professor Kwame Arhin-edited 1993 book *The Life and Work of Kwame Nkrumah*. According to Dr. Hagan, there were "those who were privileged to be involved In the great cultural self-assertion of Ghana in the sixties [1960s]."[56]

As further pointed out by Dr. Hagan, all the pro-Nkrumah workers in promoting cultural awareness in Ghana, at the time, happened to be very unanimous in carrying out then-president Nkrumah's cultural interests and enthusiasm as they supported the country's arts and its various cultural institutions. While others were championing measures of the newly independent Ghana in the area of cultural awareness, the then-prime minister Kwame Nkrumah—on April 19, 1958—used his policy address to the official delegates to a conference of such independent African nations as Ethiopia, Libya, Tunisia, Morocco, Egypt, Liberia, the Sudan, and Ghana to drum out his expectations in the cultural future of the African continent. For Nkrumah, touching on a cultural relationship among African nations should include the broadening and strengthening of such aspects as the visiting of cultural, scientific, and technical missions at both governmental and non-governmental levels; he added that the efforts should include:

> The establishment of libraries specializing in various aspects of African history and culture, which may become centers of research. There are no limits to ways

in which we on this African continent can enrich our knowledge of our past civilizations and cultural heritage through our cooperative efforts and the pooling of our scientific and technical resources.[57]

The late president Nkrumah, representing Ghana, as well as the then-president Sekou Toure of Guinea and the late president Modibo Keita of Mali, all as West African leaders, did attach a lot of importance to cultural links of their three nations. That, indeed, was why in drawing up a 1961 charter for a nucleus of African unity, their charter highlighted the impetus "to strengthen and develop ties of friendship and fraternal cooperation between the [3] member States politically, economically and culturally."[58]

Very importantly, Nkrumah, in his Pan-Africanist fervor, stressed the need for cultural awareness in the quest for African unity. Therefore, in his 1963 published book, titled *Africa Must Unite*, he—*inter alia*—also hinted on the continent's cultural heritage and decided:

To trace briefly the African background and the effects of centuries of colonialism on the political, economic and social life in Africa as a whole; to place development in Ghana in the broader context of African revolution; and to explain his political philosophy based on his conviction of the need for the freedom and unification of Africa and its islands.[59]

Nkrumah used the same book to discuss several aspects of Africa's cultural backwardness as well as the reasons for what he saw as a disorientation of African culture, as he wrote:

Our pattern of education has been aligned hitherto to the demands of British examination councils [or Boards]. Above all, it was formulated and administered by an alien administration desirous of extending its dominant ideas and thought processes to us. We were trained to be inferior copies of Englishmen [and women], caricatures to be laughed at with our pretensions to British bourgeois gentility, our grammatical faultiness and distorted standards betraying us at every turn. We were neither fish nor fowl. We were denied knowledge of our African past and informed that we had no present. What future could there be for us? We were taught to regard our culture and traditions as barbarous and primitive. Our textbooks, telling us about English history, English, geography, English ways of living. English customs, English ideas, English weather. Many of these manuals had not been altered since 1895.[60]

As a pragmatic new leader in Africa, Nkrumah sought to suggest avenues to either revise or change the course of his new nation's cultural trajectory, as he asserted, among other details:

We needed to plan an educational system that will be more in keeping with the requirements of the economic and social progress for which our new development plans are aiming.[61]

Trying to put his Pan-African cultural objective in tandem with his objective of political union, Ghana's first elected political leader pointed out that an union of African nations would raise the dignity of Africa and strengthen its overall impact on international affairs, adding: "It will make possible the full expression of the African personality."[62]

Meanwhile, Nkrumah made sure that his subordinates in his post-independent Ghana's cabinet were also in tune with his cultural awareness program. Therefore, when his education minister was, on August 20, 1957, asked to point out the new Ghana's cultural policy, under Nkrumah's leadership, promptly answered that the Nkrumah "Government is keenly interested in the preservation and demonstration of the character of the people of Ghana. The establishment of the Ghana Museum and Monuments Board and the recent opening of the Ghana National Museum are evidence of this interest."[63] Indeed, confronting Nkrumah's brand new post-1957 nation, in the context of cultural growth, were chieftaincy affairs and tribalism. That was, in fact, why he asserted the following about chiefs and chieftaincy:

> The adaptation of our chiefs to what must, for them, be distressing exigencies created by the changing relations in the national polity, has been remarkable. We could wish that other forces with vested interests might have proved as adaptable.[64]

Being very careful about tribal tendencies, Nkrumah pointed out his government's efforts toward that end:

> My government brought in the Avoidance of Discrimination Bill to deal with the control of political parties based on tribal or religious affiliations. Its full title was, An Act to prohibit organizations using or engaging in racial or religious propaganda to the detriment of any other racial or religious community, or securing the elections of persons on account of their racial or religious affiliations, or for other purposes in connection therewith.[65]

CONCLUSION

What is very unique about Ghana's late president Kwame Nkrumah was the fact that he did not set out, as a political leader, to follow a particular cultural path. Conversely, his political ambitions were mapped out by him; hence, he was prompted to urge his fellow citizens of the then Gold Coast—which became Ghana at independence on March 6, 1957—to seek the political kingdom for all other things to be added unto it; yet, as Professor Hagan confirms, "Nkrumah had laid the foundations of almost all the major cultural institutions of Ghana by the time of his overthrow (on February 24, 1966)."[66] However, Nkrumah aligned his leadership with various cultural forces, one of which being Dr. Alexander Atta Yaw (AAY) Kyerematen of the Kumasi-based National Cultural Center. In 1996 as disclosed earlier in this publication, Nkrumah, as the president of Ghana, reportedly made an impromptu visit to Kumasi, the Ashanti regional capital; the people there had played a decisive role in his electoral fortunes of the Gold Coast, indeed before Ghana's independence in 1957. Many Ashanti citizens played active roles in his successful political campaign to become Ghana's first elected prime minister (in 1957) and also as president of the new Republic of Ghana (in 1960). He was grateful to the then reigning Asantehene, Nana Sir Otumfuo Osei Agyeman Prempeh II, and his sub-chiefs for the peaceful manner in which the Ashanti Region eventually participated in the 1960 republican election. It was in Kumasi, at this time, that Nkrumah was introduced to Dr. Kyerematen of the then Ashanti Cultural Center; Nkrumah agreed to support the center financially and, subsequently, its name was changed to the National Cultural Center of Ghana on his advice, to give it a national status or character.[67]

With his thriving center, Dr. Kyerematen, after Nkrumah's overthrow in 1966, still carried out his very useful cultural work at the center, which basically continued to promote several aspect of the country's culture. It was, therefore, not surprising that when the new military government (NLC), eventually, approached him—through his fellow Adisadel College alumnus general A.A. Afrifa—he agreed to become the secretary for local government, during which he assisted the military government to institute a very strong cultural awareness program.

Subsequently, succeeding Ghanaian regimes have variously sought to promote cultural awareness in the country, often following the blueprint they inherited from earlier years. For example, former president John A. Kufuor's NPP government revised and published an elaborate cultural program that it had inherited from a national committee appointed by the National Democratic Congress regime of the late president Jerry John Rawlings. Very interestingly, professor Hagan—with unlimited cultural interests—has pointed out that in the late president Nkrumah's October 25, 1965 University of Ghana speech, titled "The African Genius," he outlined his long-standing cultural perspectives, which were meant to influence the thinking of Pan-African policy thinkers for a long time to come; it was when he was launching the new Institute of African Studies at Ghana's premier university. In the end, professor Hagan, *inter alia*, wrote about ex-president Nkrumah: "History would judge Nkrumah's cultural philosophy and strategy as a very important and necessary stimulus to the examination of how Africa would preserve and develop its cultures in a Pan-African framework."[68]

NOTES

1. A.B. Assensoh. 1978. *Kwame Nkrumah: Six Years in Exile, 1966–1972.* Devon, UK: Arthur H. Stockwell Ltd., p. 50.
2. Ibid., p. 50.
3. Ibid., p. 50; Afrifa, 1967, op. cit., p. 85.
4. Ibid, 1950.
5. Ibid., p. 50; Afrifa, Ibid., p. 96.
6. Ibid., pp. 50–51; Afrifa, Ibid., p. 96.
7. Ibid., p. 51; Afrifa, Ibid., pp. 99–100.
8. Florence Abena Dolphyne. 1991. *The Emancipation of Women: An African Perspective.* Accra, Ghana: Ghana Universities Press, pp. 45–46.
9. Ibid., p. 46; Assensoh, 1998, op. cit., p. 105.
10. Assensoh, 1998, op. cit., pp. 105–106; Kwame Arhin. 1993. *The Life and Times of Kwame Nkrumah.* Trenton, NJ: Africa World Press, pp. 207–208.
11. Ibid., p. 106.
12. Nkrumah, 1972, op. cit., p. 22; Assensoh, 1998, op. cit., p. 106.
13. Ibid., p. 26.
14. Thomas Patrick Melady and Margaret Badum Melady. 2011. *Profiles of African Leaders.* New York: Orbis Books, p.11.
15. Assensoh, 1998, op. cit., pp. 112–113.
16. Ibid., p. 113.
17. Ibid., pp. 113–114.
18. Ibid., pp. 114–115.
19. Ibid., pp. 113–114.
20. Ibid., p. 114.
21. Panaf Publishers. 1978. *Panaf Great Lives: Sekou Toure.* London: Panaf Books, p. 174.
22. Kwame Nkrumah. 1968. *Dark Days in Ghana.* London: Panaf Books, p. 19; Panaf Publishers, op. cit., p. 174.
23. Ibid., p. 174.
24. Ibid., pp. 174–175.
25. Ibid., p. 115.
26. Assensoh, 1998, op. cit., pp. 114–115.
27. Panaf Publishers, 1978, op. cit., pp. 175–176.
28. Ibid., p. 176.
29. Assensoh, 1998, op. cit., pp. 114–115.
30. Ibid., p. 21.
31. Nkrumah, 1972, op. cit., p. 112.
32. Assensoh, 1998, op. cit., p. 21.
33. Ibid., p. 22.

34. Correspondent, "Nkrumah and the Bombing Victim," *Daily Graphic* (April 16, 2015), p. 1.
35. Correspondent, "Policeman sentenced to Die for Attempt to Kill Nkrumah," *The New York Times* (April 8, 1964), international news, p. A4.
36. Ibid., p. A4.
37. Editors. 1975. *Some Essential Features of Nkrumaism*. London: Panaf Books, p. 50.
38. Ibid., p. 58.
39. Ibid., pp. 58–63.
40. Ibid., pp. 63–64.
41. Ibid., pp. 44–45.
42. Mathew R. Johnson and Jennifer Peacock. 2020. "Breaking the Bubble: Recent Graduates' Experiences with Ideological Diversity." *Journal of Diversity in Higher education.* (Volume 13: Number 1; March), p. 56.
43. Ibid., p. 56.
44. Ibid., p. 56.
45. Hadjor, 1987, op. cit., p.86.
46. Ibid., p. 87.
47. Ibid., p. 3.
48. Bankole Timothy, 1974, op cit., p. 46.
49. Ibid., p. 48.
50. Ibid., p. 49.
51. Ibid., p. 49. Also, Nkrumah's 1963 OAU founding speech is available at Ghana's National Archives. It confirms clearly that the Ghanaian leader (Nkrumah) did not have the selfish motive attributed to him by his critics.
52. Ṇkrumah, 1972, op. cit., p. 164.
53. Ibid., p. 164.
54. Bankole Timothy, 1974, op. cit., p. 46.
55. Kwame Arhin, 1993, *The Life and Work of Kwame Nkrumah*. Trenton, NJ: Africa World Press, Inc., p. 4.
56. Ibid., p. 4.
57. Nkrumah (1958 speech), cited in Kwame Arhin, op. cit., p. 4.
58. Article 3 of the 1961 Ghana, Guinea, and Mali Charter.
59. Kwame Nkrumah. 1963. *Africa Must Unite*. London: Panaf Books, Introduction.
60. Nkrumah (1963), op. cit., p. 48.
61. Nkrumah (1963), ibid., p. 49.
62. Nkrumah, ibid., p. 93.
63. Columns 5 and 6 of "Written Answers to Questions (Ghana Parliament Debates), 30th August 1957.
64. Nkrumah, 1963, op. cit., p. 84.
65. Nkrumah, ibid., p. 74.
66. Arhin, 1993, op. cit., p. 23.
67. A.B. Assensoh & Yvette M. Alex-Assensoh, unpublished Kyerematen manuscript (2021).
68. Arhin, op. cit., p. 24.

Appendix
The OAU Charter

We, the Heads of African States and Governments assembled in the City of Addis Ababa, Ethiopia, Convinced that it is the inalienable right of all people to control their own destiny, Conscious of the fact that freedom, equality, justice and dignity are essential objectives for the achievement of the legitimate aspirations of the African peoples, Conscious of our responsibility to harness the natural and human resources of our continent for the total advancement of our peoples in all spheres of human endeavor,

Inspired by a common determination to promote understanding among our peoples and cooperation among our states in response to the aspirations of our peoples for brother-hood and solidarity, in a larger unity transcending ethnic and national differences,

Convinced that, in order to translate this determination into a dynamic force in the cause of human progress, conditions for peace and security must be established and maintained,

Determined to safeguard and consolidate the hard-won independence as well as the sovereignty and territorial integrity of our states, and to fight against neocolonialism in all its forms,

Dedicated to the general progress of Africa, Persuaded that the Charter of the United Nations and the Universal Declaration of Human Rights, to the Principles of which we reaffirm our adherence, provide a solid foundation for peaceful and positive cooperation among States, Desirous that all African States should henceforth unite so that the welfare and well-being of their peoples can be assured,

Resolved to reinforce the links between our States by establishing and strengthening common institutions,

Signed:..............................

Bibliography

Adi, Hakim. 1998. *West Africans in Britain, 1900–1960: Nationalism, Pan-Africanism, and Communism.* London, UK: Lawrence and Wishart.

Ahlman, Jeffrey S. 2017. *Living With Nkrumahism: Nation State and Pan-Africanism in Ghana.* Athens, OH: Ohio University Press.

Arhin, Kwame. 1993. *The Life and Work of Kwame Nkrumah.* Trenton, NJ: Africa World Press, Inc.

Assensoh, A.B. 1998. *African Political Leadership: Jomo Kenyatta, Kwame Nkrumah, And Julius K. Nyerere.* Malabar, FL: Krieger Publishing Company.

Assensoh, A.B. 1998. *Kwame Nkrumah of Africa: His Formative Years and the Beginning of His Political Career, 1935–1948.* Devon, UK: Arthur H. Stockwell Ltd.

Assensoh, A.B. 1978. *Kwame Nkrumah: Six Years In Exile, 1966–1972.* Devon, UK: Arthur H. Stockwell Ltd.

Assensoh, A.B. & Yvette M. Alex-Assensoh. 2016. *Malcolm X And Africa.* Amherst, NY: Cambria Press.

Bangura, Karim Abdul. 2019. *Falolaism: The Epistemologies and Methodologies of Africana Knowledge*, Durham, NC: Carolina Academic Press.

Biney, Ama. 2011. *The Social and Political Thought of Kwame Nkrumah.* New York: Palgrave-Macmillan Publishers.

British Broadcasting Corporation (BBC). 2000. "Kwame Nkrumah: Man of The Millennium Award" Broadcast.

Brower, Steven, et al. 1997. *Exporting the American Gospel . . .* London, UK: Routledge.

Busia, K.A. 1964. *Purposeful Education for Africa.* The Hague, The Netherlands: Mouton & Co.

Cesaire, Aime. 1972. *Discourse on Colonialism.* New York: Monthly Review Press.

Correspondent, "Policeman Sentenced to Die for Attempt to Kill Nkrumah," *The New York Times* (April 8, 1964).

Crowder, Michael. 1984. *West Africa Under Colonial Rule*. London, UK: Hutchinson University Library.
Davidson, Basil. 1973. *Black Star: A View of the Life and Times of Kwame Nkrumah*. New York: Praeger.
Dolphyne, Florence Abena. 1991. *The Emancipation of Women: An African Perspective*. Accra, Ghana: Ghana Universities Press.
Du Bois, W.E.B. 1915. "The African Roots of the War." *The Atlantic Monthly* (May 1915).
Editors. 1975. *Some Essential Features of Nkrumaism*. London, UK: Panaf Books.
Edwards, Brent Hayes. 2003. *The Rise of Diaspora Literature, Translation and the Rise of Black Nationalism*. Cambridge, MA: Harvard University Press.
Evans, Eric J. 2017. "*Thatcher and Thatcherism*" in Stuart Hall's *Familiar Stranger*. Durham, NC: Duke University Press.
Faber, Mike. 1984. "How Nkrumah's Dream Became a Commercial Reality." *Financial Times of London* (July 18).
Falola, Toyin & Niyi Afolabi. 2008. *African Minorities In The New World*. New York and London, UK: Routledge.
Falola, Toyin & Daniel Jean-Jacques. 2016. *Nkrumah*. Santa Barbara, CA: ABC-Clio.
Hyden, Goran.
Hadjor, Kofi Buenor. 1988. *Nkrumah and Ghana: Dilemma of a Postcolonial Power*. London, UK: Kegan Paul.
Harsch, Ernest. 2015. *African Leaders of The Twentieth Century*. Athens, OH: Ohio University Press.
Hutton, Caroline, and Robin Cohen. 1975. "African Peasants and Resistance. . ." In Robin Cohen, et al., eds. *Beyond Sociology of Development*. New York: Routledge.
Hyden, Goran. 1983. *No Shortcuts to Progress*. London, UK: Heinemann.
Johnson, Mathew R. & Jennifer Peacock. 2020. "Breaking the Bubble: Recent Graduates' Experiences with Ideological Diversity," *Journal of Diversity in Higher Education* 13(1): 26–48.
Marx, Karl, et al. 1978. *The Marx-Engels Reader*. New York: Norton.
Mathurin, Owen Charles. 1976. *Henry Sylvester Williams and the Origins of Pan-Africanism, 1869–1911*. Westport, CT: Greenwood.
Mazrui, Ali Al'Amin, Ricardo Rene Laremont, and Tracia Leacock Seghatolislami. 2003. *Africanity Redefined*. Trenton, NJ: Africa World Press.
Melady, Thomas Patrick & Margaret Badum Melady. 2011. *Profiles of African Leaders*. New York: Orbis Books.
Milne, June. Editor. 1978. *Panaf Great Lives: Sekou Toure*. London, UK: Panaf Books.
Milne, June. 1974. *Panaf Great Lives: Kwame Nkrumah*. London, UK: Panaf Books.
Muller, Jerry Z. 2011. *The Mind and the Market*. New York: Alfred A. Knopf.
Murray, Charles A. 2016. *American Exceptionalism*. New York: Palgrave-Macmillan.
Ndlovu-Gatsheni, S.J. 2013. *Empire, Global Coloniality, And African Subjectivity*. New York: Berghahn Books.
Nkrumah, Kwame. 1972. *Ghana: Autobiography of Kwame Nkrumah*. New York: International Publishers.

Nkrumah, Kwame. 1963. *Africa Must Unite*. London, UK: Panaf Books.

Nkrumah, Kwame. 1968. *Dark Days in Ghana*. London, UK: Panaf Books.

Olisanwuche, Esedebe P. 1994. *Pan-Africanism: The Idea and Movement, 1776–1991*. Washington, DC: Howard University Press.

Razak, El-Alawa. 2017. *Graphic Online* (Ghana). "Opinion: Time With Cameron Duodu." (September 9).

Stovall, Tyler. 2012. *Paris Noir African Americans in the City of Light*. Boston, MA: Houghton Mufflin.

Trager, Eric. 2016. *Arab Fall . . .* Washington, DC: Georgetown University Press.

Williams, Justin. 2016. *Pan-Africanism in Ghana: African Socialism, Neoliberalism, and Globalization*. Durham, NC: Carolina Academic Press.

Zeleza, Paul Tiyambe. 2009. *Barack Obama And African Diaspora's Dialogues And Discussions*. Athens, OH: Ohio University Press.

Index

the abortive coup, xxiv
Abyssinia by Pan-Africanists, 3
Adjei Ako, xiv, 9, 14, 16, 17, 67, 68, 98
Africa in the Twenty-First Century, ii
African Americans and Caribbean-based Blacks, 16
African Americans met Blacks from the French Empire to dialogue with each other, 32
African ancestry, 29, 49
African-centeredness, 23, 27
African diaspora, ii
"The African Genius", 103
The African Governance, ii
African history, 16, 77, 100
African Interpreter, 9, 19
African leaders, xvii, xxvii, xxxiv, 13, 21, 33, 38, 40, 52, 53, 87, 88, 99, 101
African Leaders of the Twentieth Century, 23, 54
African Minorities in the New World, ix, xii, xviii, xix
The African Morning Post, xi, 87
African politics, xv, xvii
Africans and the Exiled Life, ii
Africans living on the continent, 25
African socialism, 38, 53
African states, 21, 39, 72

African Subjectivity, 52, 58
African traditional way by pouring libation, 8
the African Union (AU), 10, 22, 54
African writers, 17
Africa's development, 50
Africa to provide vanguard leadership that would result in the independence of the great majority of African countries, 37
Afrocentric intellectual cocoon, 49
Afro-pessimist, 53
Americo-Liberians, xvii, 31, 50
an ancient kingdom, 13
anti-colonialist, 26, 60
anti-colonial movements, 36
the anti-colonial struggle and the Pan-Africanist movement, 37
anti-colonial thought, 36
anti-imperialist, 26
anti-racist struggles, 26
Apaloo Assets Commission, xv, xxiii, 88
the ardent Pan-Africanist, xiii
Armed Forces, xvii, xxiii, 83, 85, 94
Asante [Ashanti], xxii
The Autobiography of Kwame Nkrumah, xxxi, 95
the awareness of Pan-Africanism, 50

Axioms of Kwame Nkrumah, xxxix

the "Back to Africa" movement, 30
Banda Kamuzu, xvii
Berlin Conference, 28
Black and oppressed, 30
Black diaspora in the 18th century, 30
Black people have historically been oppressed on the home front in Africa and in different parts of the world, 25
Black political elites, 31
Black scholars in the diaspora, 24
British Broadcasting Corporation (BBC), xviii, 97
British colonial authorities, xxxvii, 60, 61, 93
British colonial officials, xxxvii
British colonial rule, x, xii, 17, 27, 49
British drove away the Italians from power and restored Ethiopian rule, 13
the British Empire, 52, 60
the Burkinabe leader's "[Pan-African] ideas, 23
Busia, Kofi A., xv

cancer treatment at a local clinic in the capital, xxxix
capitalism, 30, 40, 81
Caribbean-born, xiii, xxxviii, 22
Catholicism's Jesuit Order, xii
The ceremonial president, xxxix
champion of African unity, 22
Chatham House of London, 15
Chief Justice Edward Akufo-Addo, xvi
Christianizing emphasis diminished as the emancipated Blacks zealously pursued Pan-Africanist ideas, 31
Christian missionaries, xi
Christian protestant churches in Pennsylvania, xii
Christian schools, xi
civilization to Africa, 30
civil rights activist Julian Bond, 66

cocoa farmers, xxii
cocoa in Ghana, 35
Colonel Ignatius Kutu Acheampong, xvi
the colonial administrators, xiv
colonial capital of London, xiii, 65
colonial Gold Coast, xi
colonial legacies that can sometimes undermine a shared African heritage, 29
colonial masters, 15
Colonial Policy, 17
colonial question and the problem of imperialism, xiii
colonization as well as imperialism and their attendant modern form known as neocolonialism, 24
the Communists, xiii
Conakry, the Guinean capital, xxxiv
The conglomeration of economic and political crises in Africa, 40
the Congo crisis, 83
continental Africans and diasporan Blacks, 16
the continent of Africa, 22, 29, 31, 33
the Convention People's Party (CPP), xiv, xxxiii, xxxvii, 60, 83, 85, 88, 94
corrupt and greedy practices, xxiii
cosmopolitan environment all of them from diverse social backgrounds, 32
coup d'etat, xiv, xvii, xxxix, 21, 72, 76, 83, 84, 88, 89, 91, 97, 98
culture, ii, xxix, 7, 18, 81
Cunard White Star Line, 6
Cushitic Kingdom of Damont, 12

the dangers of neocolonialism to Pan-African unity, 53
Dark Days in Ghana, xxxix, 90, 104
"Dawn Broadcast", xv, xxi, xxiii
Dean of the Seminary, xxxvi, 8
decolonization struggles, xiv, 25
dehumanization and outright oppression, 50
the Democrats, xiii
deregulation, 41

diaspora Blacks in the Caribbean and North America, 16
discussion in Pan-African circles on Negritude, 36
the domination and oppression of Africans on grounds of their racial and national origin, 25
DuBois's engagement with Pan-Africanism, 31
DuBois of the United States, 15, 31
Dumont, Rene, 38, 50

"Early Independent Africa's Abortive Attempt at Industrialization", xxxiv
East African leader, 10
elected leader of Ghana, 13
eliminating political opponents through killer squads and militias, 39
The Emancipation of Women, xxv, xxvi, 85, 104
Emperor Haile Selassie, xvii, 3, 13
Encyclopedia of Race and Racism, 24, 54
enslavement, xvii, 24, 28, 52
European neocolonialism and imperialism, 50
evolution of Ghana's high cultural image, xl
experience of oppression and marginalization, 24

Falolaism, 22, 27, 54
False Start in Africa, 38, 50, 56
Father Fischer, 1
Fathia Nkrumah, xxxix, xl, 92
federalism, xxii
Festus Okotie-Eboh, 14
financial liberalization, 41
the first Executive Director of the Executive Commission for Africa, 17
the first international Pan-African Congress, 52
Florence Abena Dolphyne, xxv, xxvii, 85, 104
former finance minister of Ghana under the Nkrumah regime, xvi

former Gold Coast, x, xii, xiii, xvii, 35, 94
former Senegalese president Senghor promoted to embrace Black consciousness in Africa and in the diaspora, 29
forms of solidary communities that cut across the six strands of Pan-Africanism, 29
free education in elementary and secondary schools, xv
free trade, 41
French-speaking West Africa, xvi
future African leaders, 16, 36, 97
the future leader of Ghana, 6, 16

Gbedemah K.A., 15, 63, 68, 80
George Padmore, 13–15, 22, 38
Ghana's first elected indigenous president, x, xxi
Ghana's first elected prime minister, 103
Ghana's former president Nkrumah, a leading Pan-Africanist, 49
Ghana's history, xviii
Ghana's independence is meaningless unless it is linked up with the total liberation of Africa, xviii
Ghana's National Cultural Center, xl
Ghana's president, xiv, xxi, xxiv, 70, 83
Ghana's Preventive Detention Act, 39
Ghana's year of independence (1957), xxxi
the Ghana government mostly controlled broadcasting through the issuance of licenses, 81
Ghanaian coups, xv
Ghanaian political, economic, and cultural life, 81
Global Coloniality, 52, 58
the global economy, 41, 51
globalization, ii, 54, 57
the Gold Coast students, 10
good governance, ii
governmental officials, 15

Government Teacher Training College, 5
Governor Sir Charles Arden-Clarke was sworn in as the governor-general of the new Ghana, 69
graduate studies in Philosophy and Education at the University of Pennsylvania, xii
the grave of Dr. Aggrey, 8, 9
The Great African, xxvii, 3, 4
great agitation for self-determination, 35

Haile Selassie. *See* Emperor Haile Selassie
Harvard Divinity School, 7
his Pan-Africanist ideas remain intact in the memory of Africa's peoples, 24
historically Black institution, 2
the human capital, 51
human dignity, 25, 28, 50, 51
humanities, ii
human rights, 25, 86

the idea of becoming a Catholic priest, xi
the idea of taking the vocation of priesthood, xii
the idea of West African unity, 10
ideological strata, 30
The Illusion of the Post-Colonial State, ii
impartial institutions, ii
indigenous Liberian leadership, 50
indigenous postcolonial administrations, xxii
insecurity among leaders and elected dictators, 40
internal colonialism, 50

James Emmanuel Kwegyir Aggrey education idea, 2
Jomo Kenyatta political ruling, xxxvii, 15, 36, 37, 69

the Kingdom of Punt, 12

Kirk-Greene, Anthony, xxxi
Kwame Nkrumah of Africa, xix, 4, 56
Kwame Nkrumah's Political Kingdom, 75–82

the Labor Party and the Fabian Colonial Bureau, 37
Langston Hughes Memorial Library, xxxi
the late General Afrifa, one of the architects of the coup d'etat, 83
Leader of Government Business, xiv, xxii, xxxvii, xxxviii, 63–65
the leadership of the intelligentsia, 16
leadership within African studies, ii
leaders of the foremost nationalist organization, xiv
Leninist ideas, 15
liberty of a nation, 15
The Lincolnian, 11
Lincoln Theological Seminary, xii, xxxvi, 8, 12
London School of Economics, xxxii, xxxvii, 14

Mahatma Gandhi, xxxvii, 61, 93
Malcolm X, the radical Black leader and Muslim activist, 28
Man of the millennium, xviii
The Man Who Brought Independence to Ghana, 18
Marxist and Leninist ideas, 15
Marxist vision of class analysis, inequality, and history, 30
Mazrui, Ali A., xxxi, 15, 19, 33, 40, 55
member of the Jesuit Order, xii
middle-class and reactionary intellectuals, 15
migration, ii
military dictatorship, xv
military intervention in the political process, xvii
military leaders, xiv, 39, 83
mobilization of Africa's future leaders, 16

Index

most postcolonial nations in Africa became predatory rather than developmental, 40
the movement from the perspective of Africans on the continent and Blacks in the diaspora, 36
The movement wanted to unify all African colonies and people into one nation, 34
"Mussolini Invades Ethiopia", 12

Nana Dankwa Akufo-Addo, xvi
national elections, xiv, xv
nationalism, xi, 3, 9, 12, 15, 36, 61
nationalists in Africa and radical activists in Europe and the United States, 26
the National Liberation Council (NLC), xv, xxxix
The National Liberation Movement, xxii
National Redemption Council (NRC), xvi, xl, 91
Negro History, 11
neoliberal economic policies, 41, 42
neoliberal global economy and market, 51
neoliberal globalization, 40, 42, 47
The New African, 15
new constitution for Ghana, xvi
the newest member of the British Commonwealth of Nations, 69
New Patriotic Party (NPP), 16
New York–based *Africa Watch Magazine*, 16
Nigeria's first indigenous president, xxii, 86
Nkroful in the Western Region of the Gold Coast (Ghana), xiv
Nkrumah, as the elected president, xiv
Nkrumah, Kenyatta, and other students from colonial countries of Africa in Europe, 37
Nkrumah's American and UK Sojourns, 5–18
Nkrumah's Argument With His Seminary Dean, 8–9

Nkrumah's arrival in the United Kingdom, 3, 15, 16
Nkrumah's attempts to unify the people of the Gold Coast, xxii
Nkrumah's downfall, xxiii, 99
Nkrumah's efforts impressed his fellow African leaders, 53
Nkrumah's efforts to clean house, xxiii
Nkrumah's former political opponent, xxxix
Nkrumah's London Activism And Subsequent Events, 13
Nkrumah's overthrow, xiv, xxxii, 81, 103
Nkrumah's Preparation For Gold Coast Politics, 16–17
Nkrumah's radical suggestions for unity, 53
Nkrumah's relationships, 16
Nkrumah's respect for Ethiopia, 13
Nkrumah's Student Activism In America, 9–10
Nkrumah's teaching, 11
Nkrumah and his cabinet members, xv, xxiii
Nkrumah and his future Foreign Minister, xxxvii
Nkrumah and his Nigerian mentor, 12
Nkrumah and his other Pan-African-minded African students, 59
Nkrumah and his political allies, xvi
Nkrumah and other students from the Gold Coast in Pennsylvania decided to form their own African students' association, 9
Nkrumah attended the local Roman Catholic schools, 1
Nkrumah became Leader of Government Business, xxxvii
Nkrumah encountered the political ideas and movements, 36
Nkrumah escaped unhurt, xxii
Nkrumah Leaves America For Good, 10
Nkrumah memorabilia, xxxi

Nkrumah regime to live in exile in Europe, xvi
Nkrumah suffered from pneumonia, xxxvii
Nkrumah traveled through the Port of Liverpool, xxxvi
Nkrumah used his experience to organize a Pan-African conference in 1958 in the Ghanaian capital of Accra, 37
Nkrumah was awarded his Bachelor of Arts (B.A.) degree with double majors in Sociology and Economics, xxxvi
Nkrumah was awarded the Doctor of Laws (LL.D.) honorary degree, 66
Nkrumah was forced to attack the corruption, xxi
Nkrumah went to Oxford, xxxvi
Nnamdi Azikiwe, ix–xii, xxii, xxxv, 35, 37, 86, 87
Non-Aligned movement, 53
non-radical Africans, 15
North Carolina, 8, 55
Nyerere, Julius K., 10, 33, 89

Organization for African Unity (OAU), 10
Osagyefo, v, x, xxxii, 1
overthrown in absentia, xvii

Panaf Books of London, xxxix
Panaf Great Lives, xxxii, 53, 58, 74, 104
Pan-African Congress, xxxvii, 15, 31, 34, 36, 37, 43, 52, 97
Pan-Africanism, ix, 12–14, 21–35, 37–57, 76, 90
Pan-Africanism as a broad idea, 25
Pan-Africanists are committed to the creation of a socialist society within the Pan-African milieu, 30
Pan-African movement, 10, 24, 25
partitioning of Africa into spheres of Eurocentric interests, 28

Patrice Lumumba, 24, 80, 83
people of African descent, 10
The Philosophy and Opinions of Marcus Garvey, 36
plans about how best to liberate Africa from colonial domination, xxv
political organization, 26
political organizations, xiii
political parties, xiv, 39, 102
political party members, xv
political union, 21, 102
"Politics of Confrontation", 19
postcolonial Africa, 17, 22, 23, 38–40, 51
postcolonial African nations, 41
postcolonial Ghana, ix, xxvii, 93
preaching in a Baptist Church in Philadelphia, xii
preaching in Negro churches, xii
pre-independence, xiv, 68
Preparation Toward Graduation From Lincoln University, 8
Present-day Ethiopia, 12
President Obama's election was a great source of rejuvenation of Pan-African pride and cultural efficacy, 49
prime minister, ix, xiv–xvi, xviii, xxii, xxxv, xxxvii–xxxix, 21, 41, 60, 64, 65, 68, 69, 71, 77, 79, 80, 83, 90, 100, 103
Progress Party (PP), xv, xl, 80, 89
The Promise of Development and Democratization, ii
the proverbial golden fleece, x, 5, 87
public rhetoric and discourses condemning fascism, 36

the racial hierarchies of the international system, 52
racial identity, 33, 49
racism, xvii, 25, 52
reformist in thinking, 30
regional groupings, 10
Republicans, xiii

Republic of Dahomey, 16
"A Resolution on Imperialists", 17
Revolutionary Path, 19
the revolutionary writings of Karl Marx, 36
Robert Mugabe, xvii
Roman Catholic Junior High School at Elmina, in Western Ghana, 2
the Roman Catholic religion, xi
Roman Catholic Seminary, xii
the ruling CPP's top leadership, xv
rumors that Nkrumah once entertained, xi

salvation for Africa lies in unity, 21
Sankara was assassinated, 23
scholarship on Africa, ii
School of Oriental and African Studies (SOAS) of the University of London, xxv
search for higher education in America, 6
Second World War with public rhetoric and discourses condemning fascism, 36
Secure to Africans throughout the world true civil and political rights, 31
short biographies of Nkrumah, xxxii
Sierra Leone–born journalist, 17
The Social And Political Thought of Kwame Nkrumah, xix
social institutions, 40
socialist policies, xxxii, 70
social philosophy, 11
social science, ii
social scientific traditions, ii
socio-economic arenas, ii
socio-economic links among all of the East African countries, 10
The Specter of Black Power, xxxix
structural Adjustment Program (SAP), 40
studies of Nkrumah and other Pan-African leaders, 34

subsidies, 41
surplus people, 51
sustainable and economic development, ii

Tafawa Balewa, Alhaji, xiv
teacher training education at Achimota College, xii
the Tenth Anniversary of the CPP, xxi
the theme for the fifth Pan-African Congress in Manchester, 15
the Third World, 17, 81
the time of the "Cold War" between America and the Soviet Union, xxv
Trans-Volta Togoland to become part of the Gold Coast as a Volta Region at independence, 68
Trinidad and Tobago, 13, 15, 22, 31
the Trotskyites, xiii
twin evils of colonialism and imperialism, 12
the tyranny of Jim Crow, and Africans living under colonial domination, 34

the unique contributions of UNIA members, 34
United Gold Coast Convention (UGCC), xxxvii, 16, 59
United Nations' Decade for women, xxv
unity among all the territories in West Africa, 10
unsuccessful counter-coup in Ghana, xxxix

the vision of the ideal future, 25

Western capitalist plans, xxv
Western regional governor Samuel Akintola, xiv
When Nkrumah arrived in the British capital of London in 1945, 13
the work of expeditionary forces of freed slaves, xvii

About the Authors

A.B. Assensoh is an Emeritus Professor of Indiana University and Courtesy Emeritus Professor of University of Oregon. He is the author of *African Political Leadership: Jomo Kenyatta, Kwame Nkrumah, and Julius K. Nyerere* and several other books. He is also the co-author (with Yvette M. Alex-Assensoh) of *African Military History and Politics, 1900–Present* as well as *Malcolm X: A Biography,* and *Malcolm X & Africa.* He earned his PhD in history from New York University and his Master of Law (LL.M.) degree from University of Oregon School of Law.

Yvette M. Alex-Assensoh serves as professor of political science and vice president of Equity and Inclusion at University of Oregon. She is the author and co-author of six books. In 2000, she co-edited *Black and Multiracial Politics in America* (with Lawrence J, Hanks). She received her MA and PhD degrees in political science from the Ohio State University and her Juris Doctorate (JD) degree with honors from the Maurer School of Law at Indiana University. She is an ICF-certified executive coach. The co-authors are the parents of Kwadwo Stephen Alex Assensoh and Livingston Alex Kwabena Assensoh.

www.ingramcontent.com/pod-product-compliance
Lightning Source LLC
Chambersburg PA
CBHW061717300426
44115CB00014B/2729